Holiness
J.C. Ryle
Part 2

ISBN:

Revision 0 - 14-MAY-2023

Publisher: mmlj Publishing

Email: mmljPublishing@gmail.com

Holiness - Part 2

Chapter 1 - THE FIGHT

Chapter 2 - THE COST!

Chapter 3 - GROWTH

Green wording represents MMLJ Publishing update

~~Strikeout words represent prior Victorian wording~~

1 - THE FIGHT

> **"Fight the good fight of faith. Take hold of the eternal life to which you were called, and you confessed the good confession in the sight of many witnesses"**
>
> **(1 Timothy 6:12)**

It is a curious fact that there is no subject about which most people feel such deep interest as "fighting." Young men and maidens, old men and little children, high and low, rich and poor, learned and unlearned, all feel a deep interest in wars, battles and fighting.

This is a simple fact, whatever way we may try to explain it. We should call that Englishman a dull fellow who cared nothing about the story of Waterloo, or Inkermann, or Balaclava or Lucknow. We should think that heart cold and stupid which was not moved and thrilled by the struggles at Sedan and Strasburg, and Metz, and Paris, during the war between France and Germany.

But there is another warfare of far greater importance than any war that was ever waged by humans ~~man~~. It is a warfare which concerns not two or three nations only, but every Christian man and woman born into the world.

___The warfare I speak of is the spiritual warfare. It is the fight which everyone who would be saved must fight about their ~~his~~ soul.___

This warfare, I am aware, is a thing of which many know nothing. Talk to them about it, and they are ready to set you down as a madman, an enthusiast, or a fool. And yet it is as real and true as any war the world has ever seen.

- It has its hand-to-hand conflicts and its wounds.
- It has its watchings and fatigues.
- It has its sieges and assaults.
- It has its victories and its defeats.

Above all, it has consequences which are awful, tremendous, and most peculiar. In earthly warfare the consequences to nations are often temporary and remediable. In the spiritual warfare it is very different. Of that warfare, the consequences, when the fight is over, are unchangeable and eternal.

It is of this warfare that St. Paul spoke to Timothy, when he wrote those burning words,

"Fight the good fight of faith; lay hold on eternal life."

It is of this warfare that I propose to speak in this paper. I hold the subject to be closely connected with that of sanctification and holiness. We need to ~~He that would~~ understand the nature of true holiness must know that the Christian is "a person ~~man~~ of war." <u>If we would be holy we must fight.</u>

The first thing I have to say is this: True Christianity is a fight.

True Christianity! Let us mind that word "true." There is a vast quantity of religion current in the world which is not true, genuine Christianity. It passes muster; it satisfies sleepy consciences; but it is not good money. It is not the real thing which was called Christianity eighteen hundred years ago.

There are thousands of men and women who go to churches and chapels every Sunday, and call themselves Christians.

• Their names are in the baptismal register.

• They are reckoned Christians while they live.

• They are married with a Christian marriage service.

• They mean to be buried as Christians when they die.

But you never see any "fight" about their religion! Of spiritual strife, and exertion, and conflict, and self- denial, and watching, and warring, <u>they know literally nothing at all.</u> Such Christianity may satisfy humans ~~man~~, and those who say anything against it may be thought very hard and uncharitable; but it certainly is not the Christianity of the Bible.

It is not the religion which the Lord Jesus founded, and His Apostles preached.

It is not the religion which produces real holiness. True Christianity is "a fight."

The true Christian is called to be a soldier, and must behave as such from the day of their ~~his~~ conversion to the day of their ~~his~~ death.

They are ~~He is~~ not meant to live a life of religious ease, indolence, and security.

They He must never imagine for a moment that they he can sleep and doze along the way to heaven, like one travelling in an easy carriage.

If they he takes their his standard of Christianity from the children of this world, they he may be content with such notions; but they he will find no countenance for them in the Word of God. If the Bible is the rule of their his faith and practice, they he will find their own his course laid down very plainly in this matter. They He must "fight."

With whom is the Christian soldier meant to fight?

Not with other Christians. Very unhappy Wretched indeed is that persons man's idea of religion who desires fancies that it consists in perpetual controversy!

They He who are is never satisfied unless people are he is engaged in some strife between church and church, chapel and chapel, sect and sect, faction and faction, party and party, knows nothing yet as they he ought to know. No doubt it may be absolutely needful sometimes to appeal to law courts, in order to ascertain the right interpretation of a Church's Articles, and headings rubrics, and forms formularies. But, as a general rule, the cause of sin is never so much helped as when Christians waste their strength in disagreements quarreling with one another, and spend their time in petty squabbles.

No, indeed! The principal fight of the Christian is with the world, the flesh, and the devil. These are his never-dying foes.

These are the three chief enemies against whom they he must wage war. Unless they he gets the victory over these three, all other victories are useless and vain. If they he had a nature like an angel, and were not a fallen creature, the warfare would not be so essential. But with a corrupt heart, a busy devil, and an ensnaring world, they he must either "fight" or be lost.

They ~~He~~ must fight the flesh. Even after conversion humans ~~he~~ carries within them ~~him~~ a nature prone to evil, and a heart weak and unstable as water. That heart will never be free from imperfection in this world, and it is a miserable delusion to expect it. To keep that heart from going astray, the Lord Jesus bids us **"Watch and pray, that you may not enter into temptation. The spirit indeed is willing, but the flesh is weak."** (Mark 14:38) ~~(Mark xiv. 38)~~

There is need of a daily struggle and a daily wrestling in prayer. "I keep under my body," cries St. Paul, "and bring it into subjection."'

- "I therefore run like that, not aimlessly. I fight like that, not beating the air, but I beat my body and bring it into submission, lest by any means, after I have preached to others, I myself should be disqualified" (1 Corinthians 9:26 & 27) ~~(1 Cor. ix. 27)~~

- "For I delight in God's law after the inward person, but I see a different law in my members, warring against the law of my mind, and bringing me into captivity under the law of sin which is in my members. What a wretched man I am! Who will deliver me out of the body of this death?" (Romans 7:22 thru 24) ~~(Rom. vii. 23, 24)~~

- "But the fruit of the Spirit is love, joy, peace, patience, kindness, goodness, faith gentleness, and self-control. Against such things there is no law. Those who belong to Christ have crucified the flesh with its passions and lusts." (Galatians 5:22 thru 24) ~~(Gal. v. 24)~~

- "Put to death therefore your members which are on the earth: sexual immorality, uncleanness, depraved passion, evil desire, and covetousness, which is idolatry. For these things' sake the wrath of God comes on the children of disobedience." (Colossians 3:5 & 6) ~~(Coloss. iii. 5)~~

They ~~He~~ must fight the world. The subtle influence of that mighty enemy must be daily resisted, and without a daily battle can never be overcome.

- The love of the world's good things
- the fear of the world's laughter or blame
- the secret desire to keep in with the world
- the secret wish to do as others in the world do,
- and not to run into extremes

all these are spiritual foes which trouble ~~beset~~ the Christian continually on his way to heaven, and must be conquered.

- "You adulterers and adulteresses, don't you know that friendship with the world is hostility toward God? Whoever therefore wants to be a friend of the world makes himself an enemy of God." (James 4:4) ~~(James iv. 4)~~

- "Don't love the world or the things that are in the world. If anyone loves the world, the Father's love isn't in him. For all that is in the world—the lust of the flesh, the lust of the eyes, and the pride of life—isn't the Father's, but is the world's. The world is passing away with its lusts, but he who does God's will remains forever." (1 John 2:15 thru 17) ~~(1 John ii. 15)~~

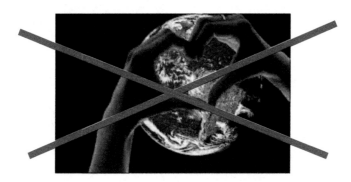

- "But far be it from me to boast except in the cross of our Lord Jesus Christ, through which the world has been crucified to me, and I to the world." (Galatians 6:14) **(Gal. vi. 14)**

- "For whatever is born of God overcomes the world. This is the victory that has overcome the world: your faith." (1 John 5:4) ~~(1 John v. 4)~~

- "Don't be conformed to this world, but be transformed by the renewing of your mind, so that you may prove what is the good, well-pleasing, and perfect will of God." (Romans 12:2) ~~(Rom. xii. 2.)~~

We ~~He~~ must fight the devil. That old enemy of humans ~~mankind~~ is not dead. Ever since the fall of Adam and Eve he has been "going

to and fro in the earth, and walking up and down in it," and striving to compass one great end - the ruin of a humans ~~man's~~ soul.

Never slumbering and never sleeping, he is always "going about as a lion seeking whom he may devour."

An unseen enemy, he is always near us, about our path and about our bed, and spying out all our ways. A "murderer and a liar" from the beginning, he labors ~~labours~~ night and day to cast us down to hell.

Sometimes by leading into superstition, sometimes by suggesting infidelity, sometimes by one kind of tactics and sometimes by another, he is always carrying on a campaign against our souls.

- Yahweh said to Satan, "Where have you come from?" Then Satan answered Yahweh, and said, "From going back and forth in the earth, and from walking up and down in it." (Job 1:7) ~~(Job i. 7)~~

- Be sober and self-controlled. Be watchful. Your adversary, the devil, walks around like a roaring lion, seeking whom he may devour. (1 Peter 5:8) ~~(1 Peter v. 8)~~

- You are of your father the devil, and you want to do the desires of your father. He was a murderer from the beginning, and doesn't stand in the truth, because there is no truth in him. When he speaks a lie, he speaks on his own; for he is a liar, and the father of lies. (John 8:44) ~~(John viii. 44)~~

- The Lord said, "Simon, Simon, behold, Satan asked to have all of you, that he might sift you as wheat. (John 8:44) ~~(Luke xxii. 31)~~

- "Put on the whole armor of God, that you may be able to stand against the wiles of the devil." (Ephesians 6:11) ~~(Ephes. vi. 11.)~~

Some people ~~men~~ may think these statements too strong. You fancy that I am going too far, and laying on the colors ~~colours~~ too much ~~thickly~~. You are secretly saying to yourself, that men and women in England may surely get to heaven without all this trouble and warfare and fighting. Listen to me for a few minutes and I will show you that I have something to say on God's behalf.

Remember the saying ~~maxim~~ of the wisest General that ever lived in England "In time of war it is the worst mistake to underrate your enemy, and try to make a little war." This Christian warfare is no light matter. Give me your attention and consider what I say.

What saith the Scripture?

- "Fight the good fight of faith. Take hold of the eternal life to which you were called, and you confessed the good confession in the sight of many witnesses" (1 Timothy 6:12) ~~(1 Tim. vi. 12)~~

- "You therefore must endure hardship as a good soldier of Christ Jesus." (2 Timothy 2:3) ~~(2 Tim. ii. 3)~~

- "Put on the whole armor of God, that you may be able to stand against the tricks ~~wiles~~ of the devil. For our wrestling is not against flesh and blood, but against the principalities, against the powers, against the world's rulers of the darkness of this age, and against the spiritual forces of wickedness in the heavenly places. Therefore put on the whole armor of God, that you may be able to withstand in the evil day, and having done all, to stand. (Ephesians 6:11-13) ~~(Ephes. vi. 11-13)~~

- "Strive to enter in by the narrow door, for many, I tell you, will seek to enter in and will not be able." (Luke 13:24) ~~(Luke xiii. 24)~~

- "Jesus answered them, "Most certainly I tell you, you seek me, not because you saw signs, but because you ate of the loaves and were filled. Don't work for the food which perishes, but for the food which remains to eternal life, which the Son of Man will give to you. For God the Father has sealed him." (John 6:26 & 27) (John vi. 27)

- "Don't think that I came to send peace on the earth. I didn't come to send peace, but a sword. For I came to set a man at odds against his father, and a daughter against her mother, and a daughter-in-law against her mother-in-law. A man's foes will be those of his own household. He who loves father or mother more than me is not worthy of me; and he who loves son or daughter more than me isn't worthy of me. He who doesn't take his cross and follow after me isn't worthy of me. He who seeks his life will lose it; and he who loses his life for my sake will find it." (Matthew 10:34 thru 39) (Matt. x. 34)

- "Then he said to them, "But now, whoever has a purse, let him take it, and likewise a bag. Whoever has none, let him sell his cloak, and buy a sword."" (Luke 22:36) (Luke xxii. 36)

- "Watch! Stand firm in the faith! Be courageous! Be strong! Let all that you do be done in love." (1 Corinthians 16:13 & 14) (1 Cor. xvi. 13)

- "I commit this instruction to you, my child Timothy, according to the prophecies which were given to you before, that by them you may wage the good warfare, holding faith and a good conscience, which some having thrust away made a shipwreck concerning the faith" (1 Timothy 1:18-19) (1 Tim. i. 18, 19)

Words such as these appear to me clear, plain, and unmistakable. They all teach one and the same great lesson, if we are willing to receive it.

That lesson is, that true Christianity is a struggle, a fight, and a warfare.

He that pretends to condemn "fighting" and teaches that we ought to sit still and "yield ourselves to God," appears to me to misunderstand their ~~his~~ Bible, and to make a great mistake.

What says the Baptismal Service of the Church of England?

No doubt that Service is uninspired, and, like every uninspired composition, it has its defects; but to the millions of people all over the globe, who profess and call themselves English Church-

men, its voice ought to speak with some weight. And what does it say? It tells us that over every new member who is admitted into the Church of England the following words are used

-"I baptize you ~~thee~~ in the name of the Father, the Son, and the Holy Ghost."

- "I sign this child with the sign of the cross, in token that hereafter they ~~he~~ shall not be ashamed to confess the faith of Christ crucified, and willingly ~~manfully to~~ fight under Christ's ~~His~~ banner against sin, the world, and the devil, and to continue Christ's faithful soldier and servant unto their ~~his~~ life's end."

Of course we all know that in countless ~~myriads of~~ cases baptism is a mere form, and that parents bring their children to the font without faith or prayer or thought, and consequently receive no blessing. The parent ~~man~~ who supposes that baptism in such cases acts mechanically, like a medicine, and that godly and ungodly, praying and prayerless parents, all alike get the same benefit for their children, must be in a strange state of mind.

But one thing, at any rate, is very certain. Every baptized Churchman is by their ~~his~~ profession a "soldier of Jesus Christ," and is pledged "to fight under His banner against sin, the world, and the devil." Whom ~~He that~~ doubts it had better take up their ~~his~~ Prayerbook, and read, mark, and learn its contents. The worst thing about many very zealous Church people ~~Churchmen~~ is their total ignorance of what their own Prayer book contains.

Whether we are Church people Churchmen or not, one thing is certain this Christian warfare is a great reality, and a subject of vast importance. It is not a matter like Church government and ceremonial, about which people men may differ, and yet reach heaven at last. Necessity is laid upon us. We must fight. There are no promises in the Lord Jesus Christ's Epistles to the Seven Churches, except to those who "overcome."

Where there is grace there will be conflict. The believer is a soldier. There is no holiness without a warfare. Saved souls will always be found to have fought a fight.

It is a fight of absolute necessity. Let us not think that in this war we can remain neutral and sit still. Such a line of action may be possible in the strife of nations, but it is utterly impossible in that conflict which concerns the soul.

- The boasted policy of noninterference

- the "masterly inactivity" which pleases so many politicians statesmen

- the plan of keeping quiet and letting things alone

all this will never do in the Christian warfare. Here at any rate no one can escape serving under the plea that they are he is "a person man of peace." To be at peace with the world, the flesh and the devil, is to be at <u>enmity with God,</u> and in the broad way that leads leadeth to destruction. We have no choice or option. We must either fight or be lost.

It is a fight of universal necessity. No rank, or class, or age, can plead exemption, or escape the battle. Ministers and people, preachers and hearers, old and young, high and low, rich and poor, gentle and simple, kings and subjects, landlords and tenants, learned and unlearned all alike must carry arms and go to war. All have by nature a heart full of pride, unbelief, sloth, worldliness, and sin. All are living in a world plague ~~beset~~ with snares, traps, and pitfalls for the soul. All have near them a busy, restless, malicious devil. All, from the queen in her palace down to the poor person ~~pauper~~ in the workhouse, all must fight, if they would be saved.

It is a fight of perpetual necessity. It admits of no breathing time, no agreement ~~armistice~~, no truce.

- On weekdays as well as on Sundays

- in private as well as in public

- at home by the family fireside as well as abroad

- in little things like management of tongue and temper, as well as in great ones like the government of kingdoms

- the Christian's warfare must unceasingly go on.

The foe we have to do with keeps no holidays, never slumbers, and never sleeps. So long as we have breath in our bodies we must keep on our armour, and remember we are on an enemy's ground. "Even on the brink of Jordan," said a dying saint, "I find Satan nibbling at my heels." **We must fight till we die.**

Let us consider well these propositions. Let us take care that our own personal religion is real, genuine, and true. <u>The saddest symptom about many so-called Christians is the utter absence of anything like conflict and fight in their Christianity.</u>

- They eat,

- they drink,

- they dress,

- they work,

- they amuse themselves,

- they get money,

- they spend money,

- they go through a scanty round of formal religious services once or twice every week.

But the great spiritual warfare

- its watchings and strugglings,

- its agonies and anxieties,

- its battles and contests

of all this they appear to know nothing at all. Let us take care that this case is not our own. The worst state of soul is "when the strong person man armed protects their keepeth the house, and their his goods are at peace", when they he leads men and women "captive at his will," and they make no resistance. The worst chains are those which are neither felt nor seen by the prisoner. (Luke 11:21) (2 Timothy 2:26) (Luke xi. 21; 2 Tim. ii. 26.)

We may take comfort about our souls if we know anything of an inward fight and conflict. It is the invariable companion of genuine Christian holiness. It is not everything, I am well aware, but it is something.

- Do we find in our heart of hearts a spiritual struggle?

- Do we feel anything of the flesh lusting against the spirit and the spirit against the flesh, so that we cannot do the things we would? (Gal. v. 17.)

- Are we conscious of two principles within us, contending for the mastery?

- Do we feel anything of war in our inward man?

Well, let us thank God for it! It is a good sign. It is strongly probable evidence of the great work of sanctification.

All true saints are soldiers.

Anything is better than indifference apathy, stagnation, deadness, and indifference. We are in a better state than many.

The most part of so-called Christians have no feeling at all. We are evidently no friends of Satan. Like the kings of this world, he wars not against his own subjects.

The very fact that he assaults us should fill our minds with hope.

I say again, let us take comfort. The child of God has two great marks about him, and of these two we have one. HE MAY BE KNOWN BY HIS INWARD WARFARE, AS WELL AS BY HIS IN-WARD PEACE.

I pass on to the second thing which I have to say in handling my subject: **True Christianity is the fight of faith.**

In this respect the Christian warfare is utterly unlike the conflicts of this world. It does not depend on the strong arm, the quick eye, or the swift foot. It is not waged with carnal weapons, but with spiritual. Faith is the hinge on which victory turns. **Success depends entirely on believing.**

A general faith in the truth of God's written Word is the primary foundation of the Christian soldier's character.

- They are He is what they are he is,
- does what they want he does,
- thinks as they think he thinks,
- acts as they act he acts,
- hopes as they hope he hopes,
- behaves as they behave he behaves,

for one simple reason They believe he believes certain propositions revealed and laid down in Holy Scripture.

"Without faith it is impossible to be well pleasing to him, for he who comes to God must believe that he exists, and that he is a rewarder of those who seek him"(Hebrew 11:6)

~~"He that cometh to God must believe that He is, and that He is a Rewarder of them that diligently seek Him." ((Heb. xi. 5.)~~

A religion without doctrine or dogma is a thing which many are fond of talking of in the present day. It sounds very fine at first. It looks very pretty at a distance. But the moment we sit down to examine and consider it,

we shall find it a simple impossibility. We might as well talk of a body without bones and tendons (sinews).

No person ~~man~~ will ever be anything or do anything in religion, unless they believe ~~he believes~~ something. Even those who profess to hold the miserable and uncomfortable views of the Deists (belief of a supreme being) are obliged to confess that they believe something. With all their bitter sneers against dogmatic theology and Christian creditability ~~credulity~~, as they call it, they themselves have a kind of faith.

As for true Christians, faith is the very backbone of their spiritual existence.

No one ever fights earnestly against the world, the flesh and the devil, unless they have carved in their ~~he has engraven on his~~ heart certain great principles which they believe ~~he believes~~. What they are they ~~he~~ may hardly know, and may certainly not be able to define or write down. But there they are, and, consciously or unconsciously, they form the roots of their ~~his~~ religion.

Wherever you see a person ~~man~~, whether rich or poor, learned or unlearned, wrestling bravely ~~manfully~~ with sin, and trying to overcome it, you may be sure there are certain great principles which that they believe ~~man believes~~. The poet who wrote the famous lines:

"For manners ~~modes~~ of faith let graceless zealots fight, They ~~He~~ can't be wrong whose life is in the right,"

was a clever person ~~man~~, but a poor divine.

There is no such thing as right living without faith and believing.

A special faith in our Lord Jesus Christ's person, work, and office, is the life, heart, and motivation ~~mainspring~~ of the Christian soldier's character.

They see ~~He sees~~ by faith an unseen Saviour, who loved them ~~him~~, gave Himself for them ~~him~~, paid his debts for them ~~him~~, bore his sins, carried his transgressions, rose again for them ~~him~~, and appears in heaven for them ~~him~~ as his Advocate at the right hand of God. They ~~He~~ sees Jesus, and clings to Him. Seeing this Saviour and trusting in Him, they feel at ~~he feels~~ peace and hope, and willingly does battle against the foes of his soul.

They will see their ~~He sees his~~ own many sins, a ~~his~~ weak heart, a tempting world, a busy devil; and if they ~~he~~ looked only at them they ~~he~~ might be in ~~well~~ despair.

- But they see ~~he sees~~ also a mighty Saviour,

- an interceding Saviour,

- a sympathizing Saviour

- His blood

- His righteousness

- His everlasting priesthood

- and they believe ~~he believes~~ that all this is their ~~his~~ own.

They see ~~He sees~~ Jesus, and casts their ~~his~~ whole weight on Him. Seeing Him they ~~he~~ cheerfully fights on, with a full confidence that they ~~he~~ will prove "more than conqueror through Him that loved him." (Romans 8:37) ~~(Rom. viii. 37.)~~

Habitual (Constant) lively faith in Christ's presence and readiness to help is the secret of the Christian soldier fighting successfully.

It must never be forgotten that faith admits of degrees. All people ~~men~~ do not believe alike, and even the same person has their ~~his~~ ebbs and flows of faith, and believes more heartily at one time than another. According to the degree of their ~~his~~ faith the Christian fights well or ill, wins victories, or suffers occasional repulses, comes off triumphant, or loses a battle.

They ~~He~~ that have the ~~has~~ most faith will always be the happiest and most comfortable soldier .

Nothing makes the anxieties of warfare sit so lightly on a person ~~man~~ as the assurance of Christ's love and continual protection.

Nothing enables them ~~him~~ to bear the fatigue of watching, struggling, and wrestling against sin, like the indwelling confidence that Christ is on their ~~his~~ side and success is sure.

- "above all, taking up the shield of faith, with which you will be able to quench all the fiery darts of the evil one." (Ephesians 6:16) ~~(Eph. vi. 16)~~

- For this cause I also suffer these things.

- "Yet I am not ashamed, for I know him whom I have believed, and I am persuaded that he is able to guard that which I have committed to him against that day." (2 Timothy 1:12) ~~(2 Tim. i. 12)~~

- "For our light affliction, which is for the moment, works for us more and more exceedingly an eternal weight of glory" (2 Corinthians 4:17) ~~(2 Cor. iv. 17)~~

- "while we don't look at the things which are seen, but at the things which are not seen. For the things which are seen are temporal, but the things which are not seen are eternal."(2 Corinthians 4:17) ~~(2 Cor. iv. 18)~~

- "I have been crucified with Christ, and it is no longer I who live, but Christ lives in me. That life which I now live in the flesh, I live by faith in the Son of God, who loved me and gave himself up for me." (Galatians 2:20) ~~(Gal ii. 20)~~

- "But far be it from me to boast except in the cross of our Lord Jesus Christ, through which the world has been crucified to me, and I to the world." (Galatians 6:14) ~~(Gal vi. 14)~~

- "For to me to live is Christ, and to die is gain." (Philippians 1:21) ~~(Phil. i.21)~~

- "Not that I speak because of lack, for I have learned in whatever state I am, to be content in it" (Philippians 4:11) ~~(Phil. iv.11)~~

- "I can do all things through Christ who strengthens me" (Philippians 4:13) ~~(Phil. iv.13)~~

- The more faith the more victory!

I think it impossible to overrate the value and importance of faith. Well may the Apostle Peter call it "precious." (2 Peter 1:1) ~~(2 Pet. i. 1.)~~ Time would fail me if I tried to recount a hundredth part of the victories which by faith Christian soldiers have obtained.

Let us take down our Bibles and read with attention the eleventh chapter of the Epistle to the Hebrews. Let us mark the long list of worthies whose names are thus recorded, from Abel down to Moses, even before Christ was born of the Virgin Mary, and brought life and immortality into full light by the Gospel. Let us note well what battles they won against the world, the flesh, and the devil. And then let us remember that believing did it all. These men looked forward to the promised Messiah. They saw Him that is invisible. "By faith the elders obtained a good report." (Hebrews 11:1 thru 27) ~~(Heb. xi. 2-27.)~~

Let us turn to the pages of early Church history. Let us see how the primitive Christians held fast their religion even unto death, and were not shaken by the fiercest persecutions of heathen Emperors. For centuries there were never wanting men like Polycarp and Ignatius, who were ready to die rather than deny Christ. Fines, and prisons, and torture, and fire, and sword, were unable to crush the spirit of the noble army of martyrs. The whole power of imperial Rome, the mistress of the world, proved unable to stamp out the religion which began with a few fishermen and publicans in Palestine! <u>And then let us remember that believing in an unseen Jesus was the Church's strength. They won their victory by faith.</u>

Let us examine the story of the Protestant Reformation. Let us study the lives of its leading champions - Wycliffe (1300's - Religious reformer that criticized the rich and power of the church), and Huss (1411 - Continued Wycliffe efforts burned at the state), and Luther (1500's - Preached doctrine of Justification by faith not works), and Ridley (1500's - Preached church should follow the Bible not human doctrine - burned at the stake by Mary the 1st), and Latimer (1500's - Preached denying the real presence of Christ in the Eucharist - burned at the stake by Mary the 1st), and Hooper (1500's - Preacher burned at the stake by Mary the 1st). Let us mark how these gallant soldiers of Christ stood firm against a host of adversaries, and were ready to die for their principles. What battles they fought!

What controversies they maintained! What contradiction they endured I what tenacity of purpose they exhibited against a world in arms! And then let us remember that believing in an unseen Jesus was the secret of their strength. They overcame by faith.

Let us consider the men who have made the greatest marks in Church history in the last hundred years. Let us observe how men like Wesley, and Whitfield, and Venn, and Romaine, stood alone in their day and generation, and revived English religion in the face of opposition from men high in office, and in the face of slander, ridicule, and persecution from nine-tenths of professing Christians in our land. Let us observe how men like William Wilberforce, and Havelock, and Hedley Vicars, have witnessed for Christ in the most difficult positions, and displayed a banner for Christ even at the regimental mess table, or on the floor of the House of Commons. Let us mark how these noble witnesses never flinched to the end, and won the respect even of their worst adversaries. And then let us remember that believing in an unseen Christ is the key to all their characters. By faith they lived, and walked, and stood, and overcame.

Would anyone live the life of a Christian soldier? Let them him pray for faith. It is the gift of God; and a gift which those who ask shall never ask for in vain. You must believe before you do. If people men do nothing in religion, it is because they do not believe. Faith is the first step toward heaven.

Would anyone fight the fight of a Christian soldier successfully and prosperously? Let them him pray for a continual increase of faith. Let them him abide in Christ, get closer to Christ, tighten their his hold on Christ every day that they live he lives. Let their

~~his~~ daily prayer be that of the disciples - "Lord, increase my faith." (Luke 17:5) ~~(Luke xvii. 5.)~~ Watch jealously over your faith, if you have any. It is the citadel of the Christian character, on which the safety of the whole fortress depends. It is the point which Satan loves to attack ~~assail~~. All lies at their ~~his~~ mercy if faith is overthrown. Here, if we love life, we must especially stand on our guard.

The last thing I have to say is this: True Christianity is a good fight.

"Good" is a curious word to apply to any warfare. All worldly war is more or less evil. No doubt it is an absolute necessity in many cases

- to procure the liberty of nations,
- to prevent the weak from being trampled down by the strong
- but still it is an evil.
- It entails an awful amount of bloodshed and suffering.
- It hurries into eternity myriads who are completely unprepared for their change.
- It calls forth the worst passions of man.
- It causes enormous waste and destruction of property.
- It fills peaceful homes with mourning widows and orphans.
- It spreads far and wide poverty, taxation, and national distress.
- It disarranges all the order of society.
- It interrupts the work of the Gospel and the growth of Christian missions.

In short, war is an immense and incalculable evil, and every praying person ~~man~~ should cry night and day, "Give peace in our time." And yet there is one warfare which is emphatically "good," and one fight in which there is no evil. That warfare is the Christian warfare. **That fight is the fight of the soul.**

Now what are the reasons why the Christian fight is a "good fight"?

What are the points in which this ~~his~~ warfare is superior to the warfare of this world? Let me examine this matter, and open it out in order. I dare not pass the subject and leave it unnoticed. I want no one to begin the life of a Christian soldier without counting the cost. I would not keep back from anyone that if they ~~he~~ would be holy and see the Lord they ~~he~~ must fight, and that the Christian fight though spiritual is real and severe. It needs courage, boldness, and perseverance.

But I want my readers to know that there is abundant encouragement, if they will only begin the battle. The Scripture does not call the Christian fight "a good fight" without reason and cause. Let me try to show what I mean.

The Christian's fight is good because fought under the best of generals.

The Leader and Commander of all believers is our Divine Saviour, the Lord Jesus Christ

- a Saviour of perfect wisdom,

- infinite love

- and almighty power.

The Captain of our salvation never fails to lead His soldiers to victory. He never makes

- any useless movements,

- never errs in judgment,

- never commits any mistake.

His eye is on all His followers, from the greatest of them even to the least. The humblest servant in His army is not forgotten. The weakest and most sickly is cared for, remembered, and kept unto salvation. The souls whom He has purchased and redeemed with His own blood are far too precious to be wasted and thrown away. Surely this is good!

The Christian's fight is good, because fought with the best of helps.

Weak as each believer is in themself ~~himself~~, the Holy Spirit dwells in them ~~him,~~ and their ~~his~~ body is a temple of the Holy Ghost. Chosen by God the Father, washed in the blood of the Son, renewed by the Spirit, they do ~~he does~~ not go a warfare at their ~~his~~ own charges, and is never alone.

God the Holy Ghost daily teaches, leads, guides, and directs them ~~him.~~ God the Father guards them ~~him~~ by His almighty power. God the Son intercedes for them ~~him~~ every moment, like Moses on the mount, while he is fighting in the valley below. A threefold cord like this can never be broken! His daily provisions and supplies never fail. His supply ~~commissariat~~ is never defective. His bread and his water are sure. Weak as they sees themself ~~he seems in himself,~~ like a worm, they are ~~he is~~ strong in the Lord to do great exploits. Surely this is good!

The Christian fight is a good fight, because fought with the best of promises.

To every believer belong exceeding great and precious promises all Yes ~~Yea~~ and Amen in Christ promises sure to be fulfilled, because made by One who cannot lie, and has power as well as will to keep His word.

- "For sin will not have dominion over you, for you are not under law, but under grace." (Romans 6:14) ~~(Rom. vi. 14)~~

- "And the God of peace will quickly crush Satan under your feet. The grace of our Lord Jesus Christ be with you." (Romans 16:20) ~~(Rom. xvi. 20)~~

- "being confident of this very thing, that he who began a good work in you will complete it until the day of Jesus Christ." (Philippians 1:6) ~~(Philip. i. 6)~~

- "When you pass through the waters, I will be with you, and through the rivers, they will not overflow you. When you walk through the fire, you will not be burned, and flame will not scorch you." (Isaiah 43:2) ~~(Isa. xliii. 2)~~

- " I give eternal life to them. They will never perish, and no one will snatch them out of my hand." (John 10:28) ~~(John x. 28)~~

- "All those whom the Father gives me will come to me. He who comes to me I will in no way throw out." (John 6:37) ~~(John vi. 37)~~

- "Be free from the love of money, content with such things as you have, for he has said, "I will in no way leave you, neither will I in any way forsake you." (Hebrews 13:5) (Heb. xiii. 5)

- "For I am persuaded that neither death, nor life, nor angels, nor principalities, nor things present, nor things to come, nor powers, nor height, nor depth, nor any other created thing will be able to separate us from God's love which is in Christ Jesus our Lord." (Romans 8:38 & 39) (Rom. viii. 38)

Words like these are worth their weight in gold!

Who does not know that promises of coming aid have cheered the defenders of besieged cities, like Lucknow (1857 - Norther India city mutiny against British rule), and raised them above their natural strength? Have we never heard that the promise of "help before night" had much to say to the mighty victory of Waterloo (1815 - British defeat of Napoleons army ending the ware)? Yet all such promises are as nothing compared to the rich treasure of believers, the eternal promises of God. Surely this is good!

The Christian's fight is a good fight, because fought with the best of issues and results.

No doubt it is a was in which there an;

- tremendous struggles,

- agonizing conflicts,

- wounds,

- bruises,

- watchings,

- fastings,

- and fatigue.

But still every believer, without exception, is "No, in all these things we are more than conquerors through him who loved us." (Romans 8:37) (Rom. viii. 37)

No soldiers of Christ are ever lost, missing, or left dead on the battlefield. No mourning will ever need to be put on, and no tears to be shed for either private or officer in the army of Christ. The muster roll, when the last evening comes, will be found precisely the same that it was in the morning. The English Guards marched out of London to the Crimean campaign a magnificent body of men; but many of the brave ~~gallant~~ fellows laid their bones in a foreign grave, and never saw London again.

Far different shall be the arrival of the Christian army in "For he was looking for the city which has foundations, whose builder and maker is God." (Hebrews 11:10) ~~(Heb. xi. 10.)~~

Not one shall be found lacking. The words of our great Captain shall be found true: "Of those whom you have given me, I have lost none." (John 18:9) ~~(John xviii. 9.)~~ Surely this is good!

The Christian's fight is good, because it does good to the soul of him that fights it.

All other wars have a bad, lowering, and demoralizing ~~demoralising~~ tendency. They call forth the worst passions of the human mind. They harden the conscience, and sap the foundations of religion and morality. The Christian warfare alone tends to call forth the best things that are left in a person ~~man~~.

-It promotes humility and charity,

-it lessens selfishness and worldliness,

-it induces a person ~~men~~ to set their affections on things above.

The old, the sick, the dying, are never known to repent of fighting Christ's battles against sin, the world, and the devil. Their only regret is that they did not begin to serve Christ long before.

The experience of that eminent saint, Philip Henry, does not stand alone. In his last days he said to his family, "I take you all to record that a life spent in the service of Christ is the happiest life that a man can spend upon earth." Surely this is good!

The Christian's fight is a good fight, because it does good to the world.

All other wars have a devastating, ravaging, and injurious effect. The march of an army through a land is an awful scourge to the inhabitants. Wherever it goes it impoverishes, wastes, and does harm. Injury to persons, property, feelings, and morals invariably accompanies it.

Far different are the effects produced by Christian soldiers. Wherever they live they are a blessing. They raise the standard of religion and morality. They invariably check the progress of drunkenness. Sabbath-breaking, wastefulness profligacy, and dishonesty. Even their enemies are obliged to respect them. Go where you please, you will rarely find that barracks and garrisons do good to the neighborhood neighbourhood. But go where you please, you will find that the presence of a few true Christians is a blessing. Surely this is good!

Finally, the Christian's fight is good, because it ends in a glorious reward for all who fight it.

Who can tell the wages that Christ will pay to all His faithful people?

Who can estimate the good things that our Divine Captain has laid up for those who confess Him before others men?

A grateful country can give to her successful warriors medals, Victoria Crosses, pensions, peerages, honours, and titles. But it can give nothing that will last and endure for ever, nothing that can be carried beyond the grave. Palaces like Blenheim (1704 - was a major battle of the War of the Spanish Succession.) and Strathfieldsay can only be enjoyed for a few years. The bravest generals and soldiers must go down one day before the King of Terrors. Better, far better, is the position of a person him who fights under Christ's banner against sin, the world, and the devil. They He may get little praise of people man while they live he lives, and go down to the grave with little honor honour; but they he shall have that which is far better, because far more enduring. They He shall have "When the chief Shepherd is revealed, you will receive the crown of glory that doesn't fade away." (Hebrews 11:10) (1 Pet. v. 4.) Surely this is good!

Let us settle it in our minds that the Christian fight is a good fight - really good, truly good, emphatically good.

- We see only part of it as yet.

- We see the struggle, but not the end;

- we see the campaign, but not the reward;

- we see the cross, but not the crown.

- We see a few humble, broken-spirited, penitent, praying people, enduring hardships and despised by the world;

- but we see not the hand of God over them,

- the face of God smiling on them,

- the kingdom of glory prepared for them.

These things are yet to be revealed. Let us not judge by appearances. There are more good things about the Christian warfare than we see.

And now let me conclude my whole subject with a few words of practical application. Our lot is cast in times when the world seems thinking of little else but battles and fighting. The iron is entering into the soul of more than one nation, and the mirth of many a fair district is clean gone. Surely in times like these a minister may fairly call on people ~~men~~ to remember their spiritual warfare. Let me say a few parting words about the great fight of the soul.

It may be you are struggling hard for the rewards of this world. Perhaps you are straining every nerve to obtain money, or place, or power, or pleasure. If that be your case, take care. Your sowing will lead to a crop of bitter disappointment. Unless you mind what you are about your latter end will be to lie down in sorrow.

Thousands have trodden the path you are pursuing, and have awoke too late to find it end in misery and eternal ruin. They have fought hard for

- wealth,

- and honor ~~honour~~,

- and office,

- and promotion,

- and turned their backs on God,

- and Christ,

- and heaven,

- and the world to come.

And what has their end been? Often, far too often, they have found out that their whole life has been a <u>grand mistake</u>.

They have tasted by bitter experience the feelings of the dying senior politician ~~statesman~~ who cried aloud in his last hours, "The battle is fought: the battle is fought: but the victory is not won."

For your own happiness' sake resolve this day to join the Lord's side. Shake off your past carelessness and unbelief. Come out from the ways of a thoughtless, unreasoning world. Take up the cross, and become a good soldier of Christ. "<u>Fight the good fight of faith,</u>" that you may be happy as well as safe.

Think what the children of this world will often do for liberty, without any religious principle. Remember how Greeks, and Romans, and Swiss, and Tyrolese, have endured the loss of all things, and even life itself, rather than bend their necks to a foreign yoke. Let their example provoke you to emulation. If people ~~men~~ can do so much for a corruptible crown, how much more should you do for one which is incorruptible! Awake to a sense of the misery of being a slave. For fife, and happiness, and liberty, arise and fight.

Fear not to begin and enlist under Christ's banner. The great Captain of your salvation rejects none that come to Him. Like David in the cave of Adullam, He is ready to receive all who apply to Him, however unworthy they may feel themselves. None who repent and believe are too bad to be enrolled in the ranks of Christ's army. All who come to Him by faith are admitted, clothed, armed, trained, and finally led on to complete victory. Fear not to begin this very day. There is yet room for you.

Fear not to go on fighting, if you once enlist. The more thorough and whole-hearted you are as a soldier, the more comfortable will you find your warfare. No doubt you will often meet with trouble, fatigue, and hard fighting, before your warfare is accomplished. But let none of these things move you. Greater is He that is for you than all they that be against you. Everlasting liberty or everlasting captivity are the alternatives before you. Choose liberty, and fight to the last.

It may be you know something of the Christian warfare, and are a tried and proved soldier already. If that be your case, accept a parting word of advice and encouragement from a fellow-soldier. Let me speak to myself as well as to you. Let us stir up our minds by way of remembrance. There are some things which we cannot remember too well.

<u>Let us remember that if we would fight successfully we must put on the whole armour of God, and never lay it aside till we die. Not a single piece of the armour can be dispensed with.</u>

- The belt ~~girdle~~ of truth,

- the breastplate of righteousness,

- the shield of faith,

- the sword of the Spirit,

- the helmet of hope

- each and all are needful.

Not a single day can we dispense with any part of this armour. Well says an old veteran in Christ's army, who died 200 years ago, "In heaven we shall appear, not in armour, but in robes of glory. But here our arms are to be worn night and day. We must walk, work, sleep in them, or else we are not true soldiers of Christ." (Gurnall's Christian Armour.)

Let us remember the solemn words of an inspired warrior, who went to his rest 1,800 years ago: "No soldier on duty entangles himself in the affairs of life, that he may please him who enrolled him as a soldier." (2 Timothy 2:4) ~~(2 Tim. ii. 4.)~~ May we never forget that saying!

Let us remember that some have seemed good soldiers for a little season, and talked loudly of what they would do, and yet turned back disgracefully in the day of battle. Let us never forget Balaam (King Balak of Moab offered him money to curse Israel), and Judas (betrayed Jesus for 30 pieces of silver), and Demas (One of Pauls "fellow workers" whom deserted them because he loved this world more), and Lot's wife (Turned to sand because she looked back when she was instructed not to by the angels destroying Sodom and Gomorrah). Whatever we are, and however weak, let us be real, genuine, true, and sincere.

Let us remember that the eye of our loving Saviour is upon us, morning, noon, and night. He will never suffer us to be tempted above that we are able to bear. He can be touched with the feeling of our infirmities, for He suffered Himself being tempted. He knows what battles and conflicts are, for He Himself was assaulted by the Prince of this world. "Having then a great high priest who has passed through the heavens, Jesus, the Son of God, let's hold tightly to our confession." (Hebrews 4:14) (Heb. iv. 14.)

Let us remember that thousands of soldiers before us have fought the same battle that we are fighting, and come off more than conquerors through Him that loved them.
They overcame by the blood of the Lamb; and so also may we. Christ's arm is quite as strong as ever, and Christ's heart is just as loving as ever. He that saved men and women before us is one who never changes. He is "Therefore he is also able to save to the uttermost those who draw near to God through him, seeing that he lives forever to make intercession for them." Then let us cast doubts and fears away. Let us "that you won't be sluggish, but imitators of those who through faith and perseverance inherited the promises." and are waiting for us to join them. (Hebrews 7:25 & 6:12) (Heb. vii. 25; vi. 12.)

Finally, let us remember that the time is short, and the coming of the Lord draws near draweth nigh. A few more battles and the last trumpet shall sound, and the Prince of Peace shall come to reign on a renewed earth. A few more struggles and conflicts, and then we shall bid an eternal good-bye to warfare, and to sin, to sorrow, and to death. Then let us fight on to the last, and never surrender. Thus saith the Captain of our salvation - "He who overcomes, I will give him these things. I will be his God, and he will be my son. But for the cowardly, unbelieving, sinners, abominable, murderers, sexually immoral, sorcerers, idolaters, and all liars, their part is in the lake that burns with fire and sulfur, which is the second death." (Revelation 21:7 & 8) (Rev. xxi. 7.)

Let me conclude all with the words of John Bunyan, in one of the most beautiful parts of Pilgrim's Progress. He is describing the end of one of his best and holiest pilgrims: - "After this it was noised abroad that Mr. Valiant-for-truth was sent for by a summons, by the same party as the others. And he had this word for a token that the summons was true, 'The pitcher was broken at the fountain.' (Ecclesiastes 12:6) (Eccl. xii. 6.)

When he understood it, he called for his friends, and told them of it. Then said he, 'I am going to my Father's house; and though with great difficulty I have got hither, yet now I do not repent me of all the troubles I have been at to arrive where I am. My sword I give to him that shall succeed me in my pilgrimage, and my courage and skill to him that can get it. My marks and scars I carry with me, to be a witness for me that I have fought His battles, who will now be my rewarder.' When the day that he must go home was come, many accompanied him to the river-side, into which, as he went down, he said, 'O death where is thy sting?' And as he went down deeper, he cried, 'O grave, where is thy victory?' So he passed over, and all the trumpets sounded for him on the other side."

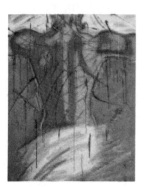

May our end be like this! May we never forget that without fighting there can be no holiness while we live, and no crown of glory when we die!

"Sanctify them in your truth. Your word is truth."

1 John 3:4

"For which of you, desiring to build a tower, doesn't first sit down and count the cost, to see if he has enough to complete it?" (Luke 14:28) ~~(Luke xiv. 28)~~

The text which heads this page is one of great importance. Few are the people who are not often obliged to ask themselves - "What does it cost?"

In buying property, in building houses, in furnishing rooms, in forming plans, in changing dwellings, in educating children, it is wise and prudent to look forward and consider. Many would save themselves much sorrow and trouble if they would only remember the question - "What does it cost?"

But there is one subject on which it is specially important to "count the cost." That subject is the salvation of our souls.

- What does it cost to be a true Christian?

- What does it cost to be a really holy person ~~man~~?

This, after all, is the grand question. For want of thought about this, thousands, after seeming to begin well, turn away from the road to heaven, and are lost for ever in hell. Let me try to say a few words which may throw light on the subject.

I will show, firstly, what it costs to be a true Christian.

I will explain, secondly, why it is of such great importance to count the cost.

I will give, in the last place, some hints which may help men to count the cost rightly.

We are living in strange times. Events are hurrying on with singular rapidity.

- We never know "what a day may bring forth";

- how much less do we know what may happen in a year!

We live in a day of great religious profession. Scores of professing Christians in every part of the land are expressing a desire for more holiness and a higher degree of spiritual life. **Yet nothing is more common than to see people receiving the Word with joy, and then after two or three years falling away, and going back to their sins.** They had not considered "what it costs" to be a really consistent believer and holy Christian.

Surely these are times when we ought often to sit down and "count the cost," and to consider the state of our souls. We must mind what we are about. If we desire to be truly holy, it is a good sign. We may thank God for putting the desire into our hearts. But still the cost ought to be counted. No doubt Christ's way to eternal life is a way of pleasantness. But it is folly to shut our eyes to the fact that His way is narrow, and the cross comes before the crown.

I have, first, to show what it costs to be a true Christian.

Let there be no mistake about my meaning. I am not examining what it costs to save a Christian's soul. I know well that it costs nothing less than the blood of the Son of God to provide an atonement, and to redeem man from hell. The price paid for our redemption was nothing less than the death of Jesus Christ on Calvary. We "for you were bought with a price. Therefore glorify God in your body and in your spirit, which are God's." "who gave himself as a ransom for all, the testimony at the proper time" (1 Corinthians 6:20 & 1 Timothy 2:6) (1 Cor. vi. 20; 1 Tim. ii. 6.)

But all this is wide of the question. The point I want to consider is another one altogether. It is what a person ~~man~~ must be ready to give up if they wish ~~he wishes~~ to be saved. It is the amount of sacrifice a person ~~man~~ must submit to if they intend ~~he intends~~ to serve Christ. It is in this sense that I raise the question, "What does it cost?" And I believe firmly that it is a most important one.

I grant freely that it costs little to be a mere outward Christian. A person ~~man~~ has only got to attend a place of worship twice on Sunday, and to be tolerably moral during the week, and they have ~~he has~~ gone as far as thousands around them ~~him~~ ever go in religion.

- All this is cheap and easy work:
- it entails no self-denial
- or self-sacrifice.

If this is saving Christianity, and will take us to heaven when we die, we must <u>alter</u> the description of the way of life, and write, "Wide is the gate and broad is the way that leads to heaven!"

But it does cost something to be a real Christian, according to the standard of the Bible.

- There are enemies to be overcome,
- battles to be fought,
- sacrifices to be made,
- an Egypt to be forsaken,

- a wilderness to be passed through,

- a cross to be carried,

- a race to be run.

Conversion is not putting a person ~~man~~ in an arm-chair and taking them ~~him~~ easily to heaven. It is the beginning of a mighty conflict, in which it costs much to win the victory. Hence arises the unspeakable importance of **"counting the cost."**

Let me try to show precisely and particularly what it costs to be a true Christian. Let us suppose that a person ~~man~~ is disposed to take service with Christ, and feels drawn and inclined to follow Him. Let us suppose that some affliction, or some sudden death, or an awakening sermon, has stirred their ~~his~~ conscience, and made them ~~him~~ feel the value of their ~~his~~ soul and desire to be a true Christian. No doubt there is everything to encourage them ~~him~~. Their ~~His~~ sins may be freely forgiven, however many and great. Their ~~His~~ heart may be completely changed, however cold and hard. Christ and the Holy Spirit, mercy and grace, are all ready for them ~~him~~. But still they ~~he~~ should count the cost. Let us see particularly, one by one, the things that their ~~his~~ religion will cost them ~~him~~.

For one thing, it will cost them ~~him~~ his <u>self-righteousness</u>. They ~~He~~ must cast away all pride and high thoughts, and conceit of their ~~his~~ own goodness. They ~~He~~ must be content to go to heaven as a poor sinner saved only by free grace, and owing all to the merit and righteousness of another. They ~~He~~ must really feel as well as say the Prayer-book words - that they have ~~he has~~ "erred and gone astray like a lost sheep," that they are ~~he has~~ "left undone the things they ~~he~~ ought to have done, and done the things they

he ought not to have done, and that there is no health within them ~~in him.~~" They ~~He~~ must be willing to give up all trust in their ~~his~~ own morality, respectability, praying, Bible-reading, church-going, and sacrament-receiving, and to **trust in nothing but Jesus Christ**.

Now this sounds hard to some. I do not wonder. "Sir," said a godly farmer ~~ploughman~~ to the well-known James Hervey, of Weston Favell (south central UK), "it is harder to deny proud self than sinful self. But it is absolutely necessary." Let us set down this item first and foremost in our account. To be a true Christian it will cost a person their ~~man his~~ self-righteousness.

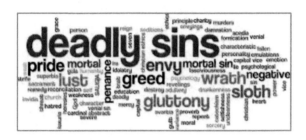

For another thing, it will cost a person their ~~man his~~ sins. They ~~He~~ must be willing to give up every habit and practice which is wrong in God's sight. They ~~He~~ must set their ~~his~~ face

- against it,

- quarrel with it,

- break off from it,

- fight with it,

- crucify it,

- and labor ~~labour~~ to keep it under, whatever the world around them ~~him~~ may say or think.

They ~~He~~ must do this honestly and fairly. There must be no separate truce with any special sin which they love ~~he loves~~. They ~~He~~ must count all sins as their ~~his~~ deadly enemies, and hate every false way.

- Whether little or great,

- whether open or secret,

- all his sins must be thoroughly renounced.

They may struggle hard with them ~~him~~ every day, and sometimes almost get the mastery over them ~~him~~. But they ~~he~~ must never give way to them. They ~~He~~ must keep up a perpetual war with their ~~his~~ sins. It is written -

"Cast away from you all your transgressions in which you have transgressed; and make yourself a new heart and a new spirit. For why will you die, house of Israel? For I have no pleasure in the death of him who dies," says the Lord Yahweh. "Therefore turn yourselves, and live!" (Ezekiel 18:31 & 32) ~~(Ezek. xviii. 31)~~

"Therefore, O king, let my counsel be acceptable to you, and break off your sins by righteousness, and your iniquities by showing mercy to the poor. Perhaps there may be a lengthening of your tranquility." (Daniel 4:27) ~~(Daniel iv. 27)~~

"When you spread out your hands, I will hide my eyes from you. Yes, when you make many prayers, I will not hear. Your hands are full of blood. Wash yourselves. Make yourself clean. Put away the evil of your doings from before my eyes. Cease to do evil. Learn to do well. Seek justice. Relieve the oppressed. Defend the fatherless. Plead for the widow." (Isiah 1:15 thru 17) ~~(Isa. i. 16.)~~

This also sounds hard. I do not wonder. Our sins are often as dear to us as our children:

- we love them,

- hug them,

- cleave to them,

- and delight in them.

To part with them is as hard as cutting off a right hand, or plucking out a right eye. But it must be done. The parting must come.

"Though wickedness is sweet in his mouth, though he hide it under his tongue, though he spare it, and will not let it go, but keep it still within his mouth" (Job 20:12 & 13) ~~(Job xx. 12, 13.)~~ yet it must be given up, if he wishes to be saved. They ~~He~~ and sin must quarrel, if they ~~he~~ and God are to be friends. Christ is willing to receive any sinners. But He will not receive them if they will stick to their sins. Let us set down that item second in our account. <u>To be a Christian it will cost a person their</u> ~~man his~~ <u>sins.</u>

For another thing, it will cost a person their ~~man his~~ love of ease. They ~~He~~ must take pains and trouble, if they ~~he~~ means to run a successful race towards heaven. They ~~He~~ must daily watch and stand on his guard, like a soldier on enemy's ground. They ~~He~~ must take heed to their behavior ~~his behaviour~~

- every hour of the day,

- in every company,

- and in every place,

- in public as well as in private,

- among strangers as well as at home.

They ~~He~~ must be careful over

- their ~~his~~ time,

- their ~~his~~ tongue,

- their ~~his~~ temper,

- their ~~his~~ thoughts,

- their ~~his~~ imagination,

- their ~~his~~ motives,

- their ~~his~~ conduct in every relation of life.

They ~~He~~ must be diligent about their ~~his~~ prayers, their ~~his~~ Bible-reading, and their ~~his~~ use of Sundays, with all their means of grace. In attending to these things they ~~he~~ may come far short of perfection; but there is none of them that they ~~he~~ can safely neglect. "The soul of the sluggard desires, and has nothing, but the desire of the diligent shall be fully satisfied." (Proverbs 13:4) ~~(Prov. xiii. 4.)~~

This also sounds hard. There is nothing we naturally dislike so much as "trouble" about our religion. We hate trouble. We secretly wish we could have a "vicarious" Christianity, and could be good by proxy, and have everything done for us. Anything that requires exertion and labor labour is entirely against the grain of our hearts. But the soul can have "**no gains without pains**." Let us set down that item third in our account. <u>To be a Christian it will cost a person their man his love of ease.</u>

In the last place, it will cost a person man the favor favour of the world. They He must be content to be thought ill of by others man if they he pleases God. They He must count it no strange thing to be

- mocked,
- ridiculed,
- slandered,
- persecuted,
- and even hated.

They He must not be surprised to find their his opinions and practices in religion despised and held up to scorn. They He must submit to be thought by many

- a fool,
- an enthusiast,
- and a fanatic
- to have their his words perverted
- and their his actions misrepresented.

In fact, they he must not marvel if some call them him mad. The Master says - "Remember the word that I said to you: 'A servant is not greater than his lord.' If they persecuted me, they will also persecute you. If they kept my word, they will also keep yours. But they will do all these things to you for my name's sake, because they don't know him who sent me. If I had not come and spoken to them, they would not have had sin; but now they have no excuse for their sin" (John 15:20 thru 22) (John xv. 20.)

I dare say this also sounds hard. We naturally dislike unjust dealing and false charges, and think it very hard to be accused without cause. We should not be flesh and blood if we did not wish to have the good opinion of our neighbors (others) neighbours. It is always unpleasant to be spoken against, and forsaken, and lied about, and to stand alone. But there is no help for it. The cup which our Master drank must be drunk by His disciples. They must be " He was despised and rejected by men, a man of suffering and acquainted with disease. He was despised as one from whom men hide their face; and we didn't respect him." (Isaiah 53:3) (Isa. lii i. 3.) Let us set down that item last in our account. To be a Christian it will cost a person ~~man~~ the favor ~~favour~~ of the world.

Such is the account of what it costs to be a true Christian. I grant the list is a heavy one. But where is the item that could be removed?

Bold indeed must that person ~~man~~ be who would dare to say that we may keep our self-righteousness, our sins, our laziness, and our love of the world, and yet be saved!

I grant it costs much to be a true Christian. But who in their ~~his~~ sound senses can doubt that it is worth any cost to have the soul saved?

When the ship is in danger of sinking, the crew think nothing of casting overboard the precious cargo.

When a limb is mortified, a person ~~man~~ will submit to any severe operation, and even to amputation, to save life.

Surely a Christian should be willing to give up anything which stands between them ~~him~~ and heaven.

<u>A religion that costs nothing is worth nothing</u>! A cheap Christianity, without a cross, will prove in the end a useless Christianity, without a crown.

I have now, in the second place, to explain why "counting the cost" is of such great importance to persons ~~man's~~ soul.

I might easily settle this question by laying down the principle, that no duty enjoined by Christ can ever be neglected without damage.

<u>I might show how many shut their eyes throughout life to the nature of saving religion, and refuse to consider what it really costs to be a Christian.</u>

I might describe how at last, when life is ebbing away, they wake up, and make a few spasmodic efforts to turn to God.

I might tell you how they find to their amazement that repentance and conversion are no such easy matters as they had supposed, and that it costs "a great sum" to be a true Christian.

They discover that habits of pride and sinful indulgence, and love of ease, and worldliness, are not so easily laid aside as they had dreamed. <u>And so, after a faint struggle, they give up in despair, and leave the world hopeless, graceless, and unfit to meet God!</u> They had flattered themselves all their days that religion would be easy work when they once took it up seriously. But they open their eyes too late, and discover for the first time that they are ruined because they never "counted the cost."

But there is one class of persons to whom especially I wish to address myself in handling this part of my subject.. It is a large class - an increasing class - and a class which in these days is in peculiar danger. Let me in a few plain words try to describe this class. It deserves our best attention.

The persons I speak of are not thoughtless about religion:

- they think a good deal about it.

- They are not ignorant of religion:

- they know the outlines of it pretty well.

But their great defect is that they are not "rooted and grounded" in their faith.

Too often they have picked up their knowledge second hand, from being in religious families, or from being trained in religious ways, but have never worked it out by their own inward experience.

Too often they have hastily taken up a profession of religion under the pressure of circumstances, from sentimental feelings, from animal excitement, or from a vague desire to do like others around them, but without any solid work of grace in their hearts. Persons like these are in a position of immense danger. They are precisely those, if Bible examples are worth anything, who need to be exhorted "to count the cost."

For want of "counting the cost" myriads of the children of Israel perished miserably in the wilderness between Egypt and Canaan. They left Egypt full of zeal and fervor ~~fervour~~, as if nothing could stop them. But when they found dangers and difficulties in the way, their courage soon cooled down. They had never reckoned on trouble. They had thought the promised land would be all before them in a few days. And so, when enemies, privations, hunger, and thirst began to try them, they murmured against Moses and God, and would fain have gone back to Egypt. In a word, they had "not counted the cost," and so lost everything, and died in their sins.

For want of "counting the cost," many of our Lord Jesus Christ's hearers went back after a time, and "At this, many of his disciples went back and walked no more with him. Jesus said therefore to the twelve, "You don't also want to go away, do you?" (John 6:66 & 67) ~~(John vi. 66.)~~

When they first saw His miracles, and heard His preaching, they thought "the kingdom of God would immediately appear." They cast in their lot with His Apostles, and followed Him without thinking of the consequences. But when they found that there were hard doctrines to be believed, and hard work to be done, and hard treatment to be borne, their fait gave way entirely, and proved to be nothing at all. In a word, they had not "counted the cost," and so made shipwreck of their profession.

For want of "counting the cost," King Herod returned to his old sins, and destroyed his soul. He liked to hear John the Baptist preach. He "observed" and honored honoured him as a just and holy man. He even "did many things" which were right and good. But when he found that he must give up his darling Herodias, his religion entirely broke down. He had not reckoned on this. He had not "counted the cost." "for Herod feared John, knowing that he was a righteous and holy man, and kept him safe. When he heard him, he did many things, and he heard him gladly." (Mark 6:20) (Mark vi. 20.)

For want of "counting the cost," Demas abandoned forsook the company of St. Paul, abandoned forsook the Gospel, abandoned forsook Christ, abandoned forsook heaven. For a long time he journeyed with the great Apostle of the Gentiles, and was actually a "fellow-laborer" "fellow-labourer". But when he found he could not have the friendship of this world as well as the friendship of God, he gave up his Christianity and opened clave to the world. "Demas hath forsaken me," says St. Paul, "having loved this present world." (2 Timothy 4:10) (2 Tim. iv. 10). He had not "counted the cost."

For want of "counting the cost," the hearers of powerful Evangelical preachers often come to miserable ends. They are stirred and excited into professing what they have not really experienced. They receive the Word with a "joy" so extravagant that it almost startles old Christians. They run for a time with such zeal and passion fervor that they seem likely to outstrip all others. They talk and work for spiritual objects with such enthusiasm that they make older believers feel ashamed. But when the novelty and freshness of their feelings is gone, a change comes over them. They prove to have been nothing more than stony-ground hearers. The description the great Master gives in the Parable of the Sower is exactly exemplified. "yet he has no root in himself, but endures for a while. When oppression or persecution arises because of the word, immediately he stumbles." (Matthew 13:21) (Matt. xiii. 21.) Little by little their zeal melts away, and their love becomes cold. By and by their seats are empty in the assembly of God's people, and they are heard of no more among Christians. And why? They had "never counted the cost."

For want of "counting the cost," hundreds of professed converts, under religious revivals, go back to the world after a time, and bring disgrace on religion. They begin with a sadly mistaken notion of what is true Christianity. They fancy it consists in nothing more than a so-called "coming to Christ," and having strong inward feelings of joy and peace. And so, when they find, after a time, that there is a cross to be carried, that our hearts are deceitful, and that there is a busy devil always near us, they cool down in disgust, and return to their old sins. And why? Because they had really never known what Bible Christianity is, They had never learned that we must "count the cost."

For want of "counting the cost," the children of religious parents often turn out ill, and bring disgrace on Christianity. Familiar from their earliest years with

- the form and theory of the Gospel
- taught even from infancy to repeat great leading texts
- accustomed every week to be instructed in the Gospel,
- or to instruct others in Sunday schools
- they often grow up professing a religion without knowing why,
- or without ever having thought seriously about it.

And then when the realities of grown up life begin to press upon them, they often astound every one by dropping all their religion, and plunging right into the world. And why? They had never thoroughly understood the sacrifices which Christianity entails. They had never been taught to "count the cost."

These are solemn and painful truths. But they are truths. They all help to show the immense importance of the subject I am now considering. They all point out the absolute necessity of pressing the subject of this paper on all who profess a desire for holiness, and of crying aloud in all the churches - "Count the Cost."

I am bold to say that it would be well if the duty of "counting the cost" were more frequently taught than it is. <u>Impatient hurry is the order of the day with many religionists</u>. Instantaneous conversions, and immediate sensible peace, are the only results they seem to care for from the Gospel. Compared with these all other things are thrown into the shade. To produce them is the grand end and object, apparently, of all their labors ~~labours~~. I **say without hesitation that such a naked, one-sided mode of teaching Christianity is mischievous in the extreme.**

Let no one mistake my meaning.

I thoroughly approve of offering people ~~men~~ a full, free, present, immediate salvation in Christ Jesus.

I thoroughly approve of urging on people ~~man~~ the possibility and the duty of immediate instantaneous conversion.

In these matters I give place to no one. But I do say that these truths ought not to be set before people ~~men~~ nakedly, singly, and alone. <u>They ought to be told honestly what it is they are taking up, if they profess a desire to come out from the world and serve Christ. They ought not to be pressed into the ranks of Christ's army without being told what the warfare entails. In a word, they should be told honestly to "count the cost."</u>

Does any one ask what our Lord Jesus Christ's practice was in this matter? Let them ~~him~~ read what St. Luke records. He tells us that on a certain occasion "Now great multitudes were going with him. He turned and said to them, "If anyone comes to me, and doesn't disregard his own father, mother, wife, children, brothers, and sisters, yes, and his own life also, he can't be my disciple. Whoever doesn't bear his own cross and come after me, can't be my disciple." (Luke 14: 25 thru 27) ~~(Luke xiv. 25-27)~~

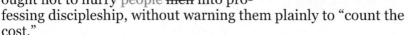

I must plainly say, that I cannot reconcile this passage with the proceedings of many modern religious teachers. And yet, to my mind, the doctrine of it is as clear as the sun at noon-day. It shows us that we ought not to hurry people ~~men~~ into professing discipleship, without warning them plainly to "count the cost."

Does any one ask what the practice of the eminent and best preachers of the Gospel has been in days gone by? I am bold to say that they have all with one mouth borne testimony to the wisdom of our Lord's dealing with the multitudes to which I have just referred. Luther, and Latimer, and Baxter, and Wesley, and Whitfield, and Berridge, and Rowland Hill, were all keenly alive to the deceitfulness of a persons man's heart. They knew full well that all is not gold that glitters, that conviction is not conversion, that feeling is not faith, that sentiment is not grace, that all blossoms do not come to fruit. "Be not deceived," was their constant cry. "Consider well what you do. Do not run before you are called. Count the cost."

If we desire to do good, let us never be ashamed of walking in the steps of our Lord Jesus Christ. Work hard if you will, and have the opportunity, for the souls of others. Press them to consider their ways. Compel them with holy violence to come in, to lay down

their arms, and to yield themselves to God. Offer them salvation, ready, free, full, immediate salvation. Press Christ and all His benefits on their acceptance. But in all your work tell the truth, and the whole truth. Be ashamed to use the vulgar arts of a recruiting sergeant serjeant. Do not speak only of the uniform, the pay, and the glory; speak also of the enemies, the battle, the armor armour, the watching, the marching, and the drill. Do not present only one side of Christianity. Do not keep back "the cross" of self-denial that must be carried, when you speak of the cross on which Christ died for our redemption. Explain fully what Christianity entails. Entreat people men to repent and come to Christ; but bid them at the same time to "count the cost."

The third and last thing which I propose to do, is to give some hints which may help people men to "count the cost" rightly.

Sorry indeed should I be if I did not say something on this branch of my subject. I have no wish to discourage any one, or to keep any one back from Christ's service. It is my heart's desire to encourage every one to go forward and take up the cross. Let us "count the cost" by all means, and count it carefully. But let us remember, that if we count rightly, **and look on all sides, there is nothing that need make us afraid.**

Let us mention some things which should always enter into our calculations in counting the cost of true Christianity. Set down honestly and fairly what you will have to give up and go through, if you become Christ's disciple. Leave nothing out. Put it all down. But then set down side by side the following sums which I am going to give you. **Do this fairly and correctly, and I am not afraid for the result.**

Count up and compare, for one thing, the profit and the loss, if you are a true-hearted and holy Christian. You may possibly lose something in this world, but you will gain the salvation of your immortal soul. It is written - "For what does it profit a man to gain the whole world and forfeit his life?" (Mark 8:36) ~~(Mark viii. 36.)~~

Count up and compare, for another thing, the praise and the blame, if you are a true-hearted and holy Christian. You may possibly be blamed by a person ~~man~~, but you will have the praise of God the Father, God the Son, and God the Holy Ghost. Your blame will come from the lips of a few erring, blind, fallible men and women. Your praise will come from the King of kings and Judge of all the earth. It is only those whom He blesses who are really blessed. It is written - "Blessed are you when people reproach you, persecute you, and say all kinds of evil against you falsely, for my sake. Rejoice, and be exceedingly glad, for great is your reward in heaven. For that is how they persecuted the prophets who were before you." (Matthew 5:11 & 12) ~~(Matt. v. 11, 12.)~~

Count up and compare, for another thing, the friends and the enemies, if you are a true-hearted and holy Christian. On the one side of you is the enmity of the devil and the wicked. On the other, you have the favor ~~favour~~ and friendship of the Lord Jesus Christ. Your enemies, at most, can only bruise your heel. They may rage loudly, and compass sea and land to work your ruin; but they cannot destroy you. Your Friend is able to save to the uttermost all them that come unto God by Him. None shall ever pluck His sheep out of His hand. It is written - "I tell you, my friends, don't be afraid of those who kill the body, and after that have no more that they can do. But I will warn you whom you should fear. Fear him who after he has killed, has power to cast into Gehenna. Yes, I tell you, fear him." (Luke 12:4 & 5) (Luke xii. 5.)

Count up and compare, for another thing, the life that now is and the life to come, if you are a true- hearted and holy Christian. The time present, no doubt, is not a time of ease. It is a time of watching and praying, fighting and struggling, believing and working. But it is only for a few years. The time future is the season of rest and refreshing. Sin shall be cast out. Satan shall be bound. And, best of all, it shall be a rest for ever. It is written - "For our light affliction, which is for the moment, works for us more and more exceedingly an eternal weight of glory, while we don't look at the things which are seen, but at the things which are not seen. For the things which are seen are temporal, but the things which are not seen are eternal." (2 Corinthians 4:17 & 18) (2 Cor. iv. 17, 18.)

Count up and compare, for another thing, the pleasures of sin and the happiness of God's service, if you are a true-hearted and holy Christian, The pleasures that the worldly people man gets by their his ways are hollow, unreal, and unsatisfying. They are like the fire of thorns, flashing and crackling for a few minutes, and then quenched for ever. The happiness that Christ gives to His people is something solid, lasting, and substantial. It is not dependent on health or circumstances. It never leaves a person man, even in death. It ends in a crown of glory that fades fadeth not away. It is written

- "Don't you know this from old time, since man was placed on earth, that the triumphing of the wicked is short, the joy of the godless but for a moment?" (Job 20:4 & 5) (Job xx. 5)

- "For as the crackling of thorns under a pot, so is the laughter of the fool. This also is vanity." (Ecclesiastes 7:6) (Eccl. vii. 6.)

But it is also written "Peace I leave with you. My peace I give to you; not as the world gives, I give to you. Don't let your heart be troubled, neither let it be fearful" (John 14:27) (John xiv. 27.)

Count up and compare, for another thing, the trouble that true Christianity entails, and the troubles that are in store for the wicked beyond the grave. Grant for a moment that:

- Bible-reading,

- and praying,

- and repenting,

- and believing,

- and holy living,

- require pains

- and self-denial.

It is all nothing compared to that "wrath to come" which is stored up for the impenitent and unbelieving.

A single day in hell will be worse than a whole life spent in carrying the cross.

The "worm that never dies, and the fire that is not quenched," are things which it passes a persons ~~man's~~ power to conceive fully or describe. It is written - "But Abraham said, 'Son, remember that you, in your lifetime, received your good things, and Lazarus, in the same way, bad things. But here he is now comforted and you are in anguish." (Luke 16:25) ~~(Luke xvi. 25.)~~

Count up and compare, in the last place, the number of those who

- turn from sin

- and the world

- and serve Christ,

- and the number of those who forsake Christ

- and return to the world.

On the one side you will find thousands - on the other you will find none. Multitudes are every year turning out of the broad way and entering the narrow. None who really enter the narrow way grow tired of it and return to the broad. The footsteps in the downward road are often to be seen turning out of it. The footsteps in the road to heaven are all one way. It is written:

- "The way of the wicked is like darkness. They don't know what they stumble over." (Proverbs 4:19) ~~(Prov. iv. 19)~~

- "Good understanding wins favor, but the way of the unfaithful is hard." (Proverbs 13:15) ~~(Prov. xiii. 15.)~~

But it is also written

- "But the path of the righteous is like the dawning light that shines more and more until the perfect day." (Proverbs 4:18) ~~(Prov. iv. 18.)~~

Such sums as these, no doubt, are often not done correctly. Not a few, I am well aware, are ever "halting between two opinions." They cannot make up their minds that it is worth while to serve Christ. The losses and gains, the advantages and disadvantages, the sorrows and the joys, the helps and the hindrances with that faith we shall set things down at their true value. Filled with that faith we shall neither add to the cross nor subtract from the crown. Our conclusions will be all correct. Our sum total will be without error.

In conclusion, let every reader of this paper think seriously, whether their ~~his~~ religion costs them ~~him~~ anything at present. Very likely it costs you nothing. Very probably it:

- neither costs you trouble,

- nor time,

- nor thought,

- nor care,

- nor pains,

- nor reading,

- nor praying,

- nor self-denial,

- nor conflict,

- nor working,

- nor labour of any kind.

<u>Now mark what I say. Such a religion as this will never save your soul.</u>

- It will never give you peace while you live, nor hope while you die.

- It will not support you in the day of affliction, nor cheer you in the hour of death.

- A religion which costs nothing is worth nothing.

- Awake before it is too late.

- Awake and repent.

- Awake and be converted.

- Awake and believe.

- Awake and pray.

Rest not till you can give a satisfactory answer to my question, "What does it cost?"

Think, if you want stirring motives for serving God, what it cost to provide a salvation for your soul.

Think how the Son of God left heaven and became Man, suffered on the cross, and lay in the grave, to pay your debt to God, and work out for you a complete redemption.

Think of all this and learn that it is no light matter to possess an immortal soul. It is worth while to take some trouble about one's soul.

Ah, lazy man or woman, is it really come to this, that you will miss heaven for lack of trouble?

Are you really determined to make shipwreck forever, from mere dislike to exertion?

Away with the cowardly, unworthy thought. Arise and play the Christian ~~man~~. Say to yourself, "Whatever it may cost, I will, at any rate, strive to enter in at the strait gate."

Look at the cross of Christ, and take fresh courage.

Look forward to death, judgment, and eternity, and be in earnest. It may cost much to be a Christian, but you may be sure it pays.

If any reader of this paper really feels that they have ~~he has~~ counted the cost, and taken up the cross, I bid them to ~~him~~ persevere and press on.

I dare say you often feel your heart faint, and are sorely tempted to give up in despair.

Your enemies seem so many, your besetting sins so strong, your friends so few, the way so steep and narrow, you hardly know what to do.

But still I say, persevere and press on.

The time is very short.
- A few more years of watching and praying,
- a few more tossings on the sea of this world,
- a few more deaths and changes,
- a few more winters and summers,
- and all will be over.

We shall have fought our last battle, and shall need to fight no more.

The presence and company of Christ will make amends for all we suffer here below. When we see as we have been seen, and look back on the journey of life, we shall wonder at our own faintness of heart.

We shall marvel that we made so much of our cross, and thought so little of our crown.

We shall marvel that in "counting the cost" we could ever doubt on which side the balance of profit lay.

Let us take courage. We are not far from home. It may cost much to be a true Christian and a consistent believer; but it pays.

I should be very sorry indeed if the language I have used above about revivals was misunderstood. To prevent this I will offer a few remarks by way of explanation.

For true revivals of religion no one can be more deeply thankful than I am. Wherever they may take place, and by whatever agents they may be effected, I desire to bless God for them, with all my heart.

"If Christ is preached," I rejoice, whoever may be the preacher.

If souls are saved, I rejoice, by whatever section of the Church the word of life has been ministered.

But it is a melancholy fact that, in a world like this, you cannot have good without evil. I have no hesitation in saying, that one consequence of the revival movement has been the rise of a theological system which I feel obliged to call defective and mischievous in the extreme. The leading feature of the theological system I refer to, is this an extravagant and disproportionate magnifying of three points in religion,

- instantaneous conversion

- the invitation of unconverted sinners to come to Christ,

- and the possession of inward joy and peace as a test of conversion.

I repeat that these three grand truths (for truths they are) are so incessantly and exclusively brought forward, in some quarters, that great harm is done.

Instantaneous conversion, no doubt, ought to be pressed on people. But surely they ought not to be led to suppose that there is no other sort of conversion, and that unless they are suddenly and powerfully converted to God, they are not converted at all.

The duty of coming to Christ at once, "**just as we are**," should be pressed on all hearers. It is the very corner-stone of Gospel preaching.

But surely people men ought to be told to repent as well as to believe.

They should be told why they are to come to Christ, and what they are to come for, and whence their need arises. The nearness of peace and comfort in Christ should be proclaimed to all ~~men~~.

But surely they should be taught that the possession of strong inward joys and high frames of mind is not essential to justification, and that there may be true faith and true peace without such very triumphant feelings.

<u>Joy alone is no certain evidence of grace.</u> The defects of the theological system I have in view appear to me to be these:

(1) The work of the Holy Ghost in converting sinners is far too much narrowed and confined to one single way. Not all true converts are converted instantaneously, like Saul and the Philippian jailor.

(2) Sinners are not sufficiently instructed about the holiness of God's law, the depth of their sinfulness, and the real guilt of sin. To be incessantly telling a sinner to "come to Christ" is of little use, unless you tell them ~~him~~ why they need ~~he needs~~ to come, and show them ~~him~~ fully their ~~his~~ sins.

(3) Faith is not properly explained. In some cases people are taught that mere feeling is faith. In others they are taught that if they believe that Christ died for sinners they have faith! At this rate the very devils are believers!

(4) The possession of inward joy and assurance is made essential to believing. Yet assurance is certainly not of the essence of saving faith. There may be faith when there is no assurance. To insist on all believers at once "rejoicing," as soon as they believe, is most unsafe. Some, I am quite sure, will rejoice without believing, while others will believe who cannot at once rejoice.

(5) Last, but not least, the sovereignty of God in saving sinners, and the absolute necessity of preventing grace, are far too much overlooked. Many talk as if conversions could be manufactured at a persons ~~man's~~ pleasure, and as if there were no such text as this, "So then it is not of him who wills, nor of him who runs, but of God who has mercy." (Romans 9:16) ~~(Rom. ix. 16.)~~

The mischief done by the theological system I refer to is, I am persuaded, very great. On the one hand, many humble minded Christians are totally discouraged and daunted. They fancy they have no grace because they cannot reach up to the high frames and feelings which are pressed on their attention.

On the other side, many grace-less people are deluded into thinking they are "converted," because under the pressure or animal excitement and tempo-rary feelings they arc led to profess themselves Christians.

And all this time the thoughtless and ungodly look on with con-tempt, and rind fresh reasons for neglecting religion altogether.

The antidotes to the state of things I deplore are plain and few.

(1) Let "all the counsel of God be taught" in Scriptural proportion; and let not two or three precious doctrines of the Gospel be al-lowed to overshadow all other truths.

(2) Let repentance be taught fully as well as faith, and not thrust completely into the background. Our Lord Jesus Christ and St. Paul always taught both.

(3) Let the variety of the Holy Ghost's works be honestly stated and admitted; and while instantaneous conversion is pressed on people men, let it not be taught as a necessity.

(4) Let those who profess to have found immediate sensible peace be plainly warned to try themselves well, and to remember that feeling is not faith, and that "If you remain in my word, then you are truly my disciples" is the great pro of that faith is true. (John 8:31) (John viii. 31.)

(5) Let the great duty of "counting the cost" be constantly urged on all who are disposed to make a religious profession, and let them be honestly and fairly told that there is warfare as well as peace, a cross as well as a crown, in Christ's service.

I am sure that unhealthy excitement is above all things to be dreaded in religion, because it often ends in fatal, soul ruining re-action and utter deadness. And when multitudes are suddenly brought under the power of religious impressions, unhealthy ex-citement is almost sure to follow.

I have not much faith in the soundness of conversions when they are said to take places in masses and wholesale. It does not seem to me in harmony with God's general dealings in this dispensation.

To my eyes it appears that God's ordinary plan is to call in individuals one by one.

Therefore, when I hear of large numbers being suddenly converted all at one time, I hear of it with less hope than some. The healthiest and most enduring success in mission fields is certainly not where natives have come over to Christianity in a mass.

The most satisfactory and firmest work at home does not always appear to me to be the work done in revivals.

There are two passages of Scripture which I should like to have frequently and fully expounded in the present day by all who preach the Gospel, and specially by those who have anything to do with revivals.

One passage is the parable of the sower, That parable is not recorded three times over without good reason and a deep meaning.

The other passage is our Lord's teaching about "counting the cost," and the words which He spoke to the "great multitudes" whom He saw following Him. It is very noteworthy that He did not on that occasion say anything to flatter these volunteers or encourage them to follow Him. No: He saw what their case needed. He told them to stand still and "count the cost."

"For which of you, desiring to build a tower, doesn't first sit down and count the cost, to see if he has enough to complete it? Or perhaps, when he has laid a foundation and isn't able to finish, everyone who sees begins to mock him" (Luke 14:28 & 29) (Luke xiv. 28, etc.)

I am not sure that some modern preachers would have adopted this course of treatment.

3 - GROWTH

> ### "But don't forget this one thing, beloved, that one day is with the Lord as a thousand years, and a thousand years as one day."
>
> *2 Peter 3:8*

The subject of the text which heads this page is one which I dare not omit in this volume about Holiness. It is one that ought to be deeply interesting to every true Christian. It naturally raises the questions,

Do we grow in grace?

Do we get on in our religion?

Do we make progress?

To a mere formal Christian I cannot expect the inquiry to seem worth attention. The person whom ~~man who~~ has nothing more than a kind of Sunday religion whose Christianity is like their ~~his~~ Sunday clothes, put on once a week, and then laid aside such a person ~~man~~ cannot, of course, be expected to care about "growth in grace."

They know ~~He knows~~ nothing about such matters.

"Now the natural man doesn't receive the things of God's Spirit, for they are foolishness to him; and he can't know them, because they are spiritually discerned." (1 Corinthians 2:14) ~~(1 Cor. ii. 14.)~~

But to every one who is in down-right earnest about their ~~his~~ soul, and hungers and thirsts after spiritual life, the question ought to come home with searching power. **Do we make progress in our religion? Do we grow?**

The question is one that is always useful, but especially so at certain seasons.

- A Saturday night,

- a Communion Sunday,

- the return of a birthday,

- the end of a year

all these are seasons that ought to set us thinking, and make us look within.

- Time is fast flying.

- Life is fast receding ~~ebbing~~ away.

The hour is daily drawing nearer when the reality of our Christianity will be tested, and it will be seen whether we have built on "the rock" or on "the sand." Surely it becomes us from time to time to examine ourselves, and take account of our souls? **Do we get on in spiritual things? Do we grow?**

The question is one that is of special importance in the present day. Crude and strange opinions are floating in peoples ~~men's~~ minds on some points of doctrine, and among others on the point of "growth in grace," as an essential part of true holiness.

By some it is totally denied. By others it is explained away, and pared down to nothing. By thousands it is misunderstood, and consequently neglected. In a day like this it is useful to look fairly in the face the whole subject of Christian growth.

In considering this subject there are three things which I wish to bring forward and establish:

1) <u>The reality of religious growth</u>. There is such a thing as "growth in grace."

2) <u>The marks of religious growth.</u> There are marks by which "growth in grace" may be known.

3) <u>The means of religious growth.</u> There are means that must be used by those who desire "growth in grace."

I know not who you are, into whose hands this paper may have fallen. But I am not ashamed to ask your best attention to its contents. Believe me, the subject is no mere matter of speculation and controversy. It is an eminently practical subject, if any is in religion. It is intimately and inseparably connected with the whole question of "sanctification." It is a leading mark of true saints that they grow.

The spiritual health and prosperity, the spiritual happiness and comfort of every true-hearted and holy Christian, are intimately connected with the subject of spiritual growth.

<u>The first point I propose to establish is this: There is such a thing as growth in grace.</u>

That any Christian should deny this proposition is at first sight a strange and melancholy thing. But it is fair to remember that a person ~~man's~~ understanding is fallen no less than their ~~his~~ will.

Disagreements about doctrines are often nothing more than disagreements about the meaning of words. I try to hope that it is so in the present case.

I try to believe that when I speak of "growth in grace" and maintain it, I mean one thing, while my brethren who deny it mean quite another. Let me therefore clear the way by explaining what I mean.

When I speak of "growth in grace,"

- I do not for a moment mean that a believer's interest in Christ can grow.

- I do not mean that they ~~he~~ can grow in safety, acceptance with God, or security.

- I do not mean that they ~~he~~ can ever be more justified, more pardoned, more forgiven, more at peace with God, than they are ~~he is~~ the first moment that they ~~he~~ believes.

- I hold firmly that the justification of a believer is a finished, perfect, and complete work; and that the weakest saint, though they ~~he~~ may not know and feel it, is as completely justified as the strongest.

- I hold firmly that our election, calling, and standing in Christ admit of no degrees, increase, or diminution. If any one dreams that by "growth in grace" I mean growth in. justification they are ~~he is~~ utterly wide of the mark, and utterly mistaken about the whole point I am considering. I would go to the stake, God helping me, for the glorious truth, that in the matter of justification before God every believer is "and in him you are made full, who is the head of all principality and power." (Colossians 2:10) ~~(Col. ii. 10.)~~

- Nothing can be added to their ~~his~~ justification from the moment they believe ~~he believes~~, and nothing taken away.

When I speak of "growth in grace" I only mean increase in the degree, size, strength, vigor ~~vigour~~, and power of the graces which the Holy Spirit plants in a believer's heart.

I hold that every one of those graces admits of growth, progress, and increase.

I hold that repentance, faith, hope, love, humility, zeal, courage, and the like, may be little or great, strong or weak, vigorous or feeble, and may vary greatly in the same person ~~man~~ at different periods of their ~~his~~ life.

When I speak of a persons ~~man~~ "growing in grace," I mean simply this

- that their ~~his~~ sense of sin is becoming deeper,

- their ~~his~~ faith stronger,

- their ~~his~~ hope brighter,

- their ~~his~~ love more extensive,

- their his spiritual-mindedness more marked.

They feel ~~He feels~~ more of the power of godliness in their ~~his~~ own heart. They ~~He~~ manifests more of it in their ~~his~~ life. They are ~~He is~~ going on from strength to strength, from faith to faith, and from grace to grace. I leave it to others to describe such a persons ~~man's~~ condition by any words they please. For myself I think the truest and best account of them ~~him~~ is this - their ~~he is~~ "growing in grace."

One principal ground on which I build this doctrine of "growth in grace," is the plain language of Scripture. If words in the Bible mean anything, there is such a thing as "growth," and believers ought to be exhorted to "grow." -

What says St. Paul?

- "We are bound to always give thanks to God for you, brothers, even as it is appropriate, because your faith grows exceedingly, and the love of each and every one of you toward one another abounds" (2 Thessalonians 1:3) ~~(2 Thess. i. 3)~~

- "for indeed you do it toward all the brothers who are in all Macedonia. But we exhort you, brothers, that you abound more and more" (1 Thessalonians 4:10) ~~(1 Thess. iv. 10.)~~

- "For this cause, we also, since the day we heard this, don't cease praying and making requests for you, that you may be filled with the knowledge of his will in all spiritual wisdom and understanding, that you may walk worthily of the Lord, to please him in all respects, bearing fruit in every good work and increasing in the knowledge of God" (Colossians 1:9 & 10) ~~(Col. i 10.)~~

- "not boasting beyond proper limits in other men's labors, but having hope that as your faith grows, we will be abundantly enlarged by you in our sphere of influence" (1 Corinthians 10:15) ~~(2 Cor. x. 15.)~~

- "May the Lord make you to increase and abound in love toward one another and toward all men, even as we also do toward you" (1 Thessalonians 3:12) ~~(1 Thess. iii. 12.)~~

- "but speaking truth in love, we may grow up in all things into him who is the head, Christ" (Ephesians 4:15) ~~(Eph. iv. 15.)~~

- "This I pray, that your love may abound yet more and more in knowledge and all discernment" (Philippians 1:9) ~~(Phil. i. 9.)~~

- "'Finally then, brothers, we beg and exhort you in the Lord Jesus, that as you received from us how you ought to walk and to please God, that you abound more and more." (1 Thessalonians 4:1) (~~1 Thess. iv. 1.~~)

- What says St. Peter? "Putting away therefore all wickedness, all deceit, hypocrisies, envies, and all evil speaking, as newborn babies, long for the pure spiritual milk, that with it you may grow, if indeed you have tasted that the Lord is gracious." (1 Peter 2:1 thru 3) (~~1 Pet. ii. 2.~~)

- "But grow in the grace and knowledge of our Lord and Savior Jesus Christ. To him be the glory both now and forever. Amen." (2 Peter 3:18) (~~2 Pet. iii. 18.~~)

I know not what others think of such texts. To me they seem to establish the doctrine for which I contend, and to be incapable of any other explanation. Growth in grace is taught in the Bible. I might stop here and say no more.

The other ground, however, on which I build the doctrine of "growth in grace," is the ground of fact and experience.

I ask any honest reader of the New Testament whether they ~~he~~ cannot see degrees of grace in the New Testament saints whose histories are recorded, as plainly as the sun at noon-day?

I ask them ~~him~~ whether they ~~he~~ cannot see in the very same persons as great a difference between their faith and knowledge at one time and at another, as between the same persons ~~man's~~ strength when their ~~he is~~ an infant and when their ~~he is~~ a grownup person ~~man~~?

I ask them ~~him~~ whether the Scripture does not distinctly recognize ~~recognise~~ this in the language it uses, when it speaks of "weak" faith and "strong" faith, and of Christians as "new-born babes," "little children," "young men," and "fathers "? (1 Peter 2:2 & John 2:12 thru 14) ~~(1 Pet. ii. 2; John ii. 12-14.)~~

- I ask them ~~him,~~ above all, whether their ~~his~~ own observation of believers, now-a-days, does not bring them ~~him~~ to the same conclusion?
- What true Christian would not confess that there is as much difference between the degree of their ~~his~~ own faith and knowledge when they were ~~he was~~ first converted, and their ~~his~~ present attainments, as there is between a sapling and a full-grown tree?
- Their ~~His~~ graces are the same in principle; but they have grown.

I know not how these facts strike others: to my eyes they seem to prove, most unanswerably, **that "growth in grace" is a real thing**.

I feel almost ashamed to dwell so long upon this part of my subject. In fact, if any Christian ~~man~~ means to say that the faith, and hope, and knowledge, and holiness of a newly-converted person, are as strong as those of an old-established believer, and need no increase, it is waste of time to argue further.

No doubt they are as real, but not so strong

- as true, but not so vigorous
- as much seeds of the Spirit's planting,
- but not yet so fruitful.

And if any one asks how they are to become stronger, I say it must be by the same process by which all things having life increase - **they must grow. And this is what I mean by "growth in grace."**

Let us turn away from the things I have been discussing to a more practical view of the great subject before us. I want Christians ~~men~~ to look at "growth in grace" as a thing of infinite importance to the soul. I believe, whatever others may think, that our best interests are concerned in a right view of the question - **Do we grow?**

Let us know then that "growth in grace" is the best evidence of spiritual health and prosperity. In a child, or a flower, or a tree, we are all aware that when there is no growth there is something wrong.

Healthy life in an animal or vegetable will always show itself by progress and increase. It is just the same with our souls. **If they are progressing and doing well they will grow.**

Baby Girl Growth Chart For 0 to 12 Months		
Age (Months)	Weight (kg) 3rd to 97th percentile	Height (cm) 3rd to 97th percentile
0	2.4 - 4.2	45.6 - 52.7
1	3.2 - 5.4	50.0 - 57.4
2	4.0 - 6.5	53.2 - 60.9
3	4.6 - 7.4	55.8 - 63.8
4	5.1 - 8.1	58.0 - 66.2
5	5.5 - 8.7	59.9 - 68.2
6	5.8 - 9.2	61.5 - 70.0
7	6.1 - 9.6	62.9 - 71.6
8	6.3 - 10.0	64.3 - 73.2
9	6.6 - 10.4	65.6 - 74.7
10	6.8 - 10.7	66.8 - 76.1
11	7.0 - 11.0	68.0 - 77.5
12	7.1 - 11.3	69.2 - 78.9

Let us know, furthermore, that "growth in grace" is one way to be happy in our religion. God has wisely linked together our comfort and our increase in holiness. He has graciously made it our interest to press on and aim high in our Christianity. There is a vast difference between the amount of sensible enjoyment which one believer has in their ~~his~~ religion compared to another. But you may be sure that ordinarily the person ~~man~~ who feels the most "joy and peace in believing," and has the clearest witness of the Spirit in their ~~his~~ heart, is the Christian ~~man~~ who grows.

Let us know, furthermore, that "growth in grace" is one secret of usefulness to others. Our influence on others for good depends greatly on what they see in us. The children of the world measure Christianity quite as much by their eyes as by their ears. The Christian who is always at a standstill, to all appearances the same person ~~man~~, with the same little faults, and weaknesses, and besetting sins, and petty infirmities, is seldom the Christian who does much good. The Christian ~~man~~ who shakes and stirs minds, and sets the world thinking, is the believer who is continually improving and going forward. People ~~Men~~ think there is life and reality when they see growth.

Let us know, furthermore, that "growth in grace" pleases God. It may seem a wonderful thing, no doubt, that anything done by such creatures as we are can give pleasure to the Most High God. But so it is. The Scripture speaks of walking so as to "please God." The Scripture says there are sacrifices with which

- "Finally then, brothers, we beg and exhort you in the Lord Jesus, that as you received from us how you ought to walk and to please God, that you abound more and more." (1 Thessalonians 4:1) ~~(1 Thess. iv. 1.)~~
- "But don't forget to be doing good and sharing, for with such sacrifices God is well pleased." (Hebrews 13:16) ~~(Heb. xiii. 16.)~~

A person ~~The husband man~~ loves to see the plants on which they have planted ~~he has bestowed labour~~ flourishing and bearing fruit. It cannot but disappoint and grieve them ~~him~~ to see they are ~~them~~ stunted and standing still.

Now what does our Lord Himself say?

- "I am the true vine, and my Father is the farmer" & "In this my Father is glorified, that you bear much fruit; and so you will be my disciples." (John 15:1 & 8) ~~(John xv. 1, 8.)~~

The Lord takes pleasure in all His people - but specially in those that grow.

Let us know, above all, that "growth in grace" is not only a thing possible, but a thing for which believers are accountable.

- To tell an unconverted person ~~man~~, dead in sins, to "grow in grace" would doubtless be absurd.
- To tell a believer, who is quickened and alive to God, to grow, is only summoning them ~~him~~ to a plain Scriptural duty. They have ~~He has~~ a new principle within them ~~him~~, and it is a solemn duty not to quench it. Neglect of growth robs them ~~him~~ of privileges, grieves the Spirit, and makes the chariot wheels of their ~~his~~ soul move heavily. Whose fault is it, I should like to know, if a believer does not grow in grace?

The fault, I am sure, cannot be laid on God. He delights to:

"But he gives more grace. Therefore it says, "God resists the proud, but gives grace to the humble."" (James 4:6) (James iv. 6)

"Let those who favor my righteous cause shout for joy and be glad. Yes, let them say continually, "May Yahweh be magnified, who has pleasure in the prosperity of his servant!"" (Psalms 35:27) (Psa. v. 27.)

The fault, no doubt, is our own. We ourselves are to blame, and none else, if we do not grow.

The second point I propose to establish is this: There are marks by which growth in grace may be known.

Let me take it for granted that we do not question the reality of growth in grace and its vast importance. - So far so good.

But you now want to know how anyone may find out whether they are he is growing in grace or not? I answer that question, in the first place, observing that we are very poor judges of our own condition, and that bystanders often know us better than we know ourselves. But I answer further, that there are undoubtedly certain great marks and signs of growth in grace, and that wherever you see these marks you see a "growing" soul. I will now proceed to place some of these marks before you in order.

One mark of "growth in grace" is increased humility. The person man whose soul is "growing," feels their his own sinfulness and unworthiness more every year. They are He is ready to say with

- Job "Then Job answered Yahweh, "Behold, I am of small account. What will I answer you? I lay my hand on my mouth. I have spoken once, and I will not answer; Yes, twice, but I will proceed no further."" (Job 40:3 thru 5) (Job xl. 4)

- and with Abraham, "...I am dust and ashes." (Genesis 18:27) (Gen. xviii. 27)

- and with Jacob, "I am not worthy of the least of all the loving kindnesses, and of all the truth, which you have shown to your servant..." (Psalms 32:10) ~~(Ps. xxxii. 10)~~

- and with David, "But I am a worm" (Psalms 22:6) ~~(Ps. xxii. 6)~~

- and with Isaiah, "Then I said, "Woe is me! For I am undone, because I am a man of unclean lips and I live among a people of unclean lips, for my eyes have seen the King, Yahweh of Armies!" I am a man of unclean lips," (Isaiah 6:5) ~~(Isa. vi. 5)~~

- and with Peter, "But Simon Peter, when he saw it, fell down at Jesus' knees, saying, "Depart from me, for I am a sinful man, Lord." (Luke 5:8) ~~(Luke v. 8.)~~

The nearer they draw ~~he draws~~ to God, and the more they see ~~he sees~~ of God's holiness and perfection, the more thoroughly is their ~~he~~ sensible of their ~~his~~ own countless imperfections. The further they ~~he~~ journeys in the way to heaven, the more they understand ~~he understands~~ what St. Paul means when he says,

-"Not that I have already obtained, or am already made perfect; but I press on, that I may take hold of that for which also I was taken hold of by Christ Jesus." (Philippians 3:12) ~~(Phil. iii. 12)~~

- "For I am the least of the apostles, who is not worthy to be called an apostle, because I persecuted the assembly of God." (1 Corinthians 15:9) ~~(1 Cor. xv. 9)~~

- "To me, the very least of all saints, was this grace given, to preach to the Gentiles the unsearchable riches of Christ" (Ephesians 3:8) ~~(Ephes. iii. 8)~~

- "The saying is faithful and worthy of all acceptance, that Christ Jesus came into the world to save sinners, of whom I am chief." (1 Timothy 1:15) ~~(1 Tim. i. 15.)~~

The riper they are ~~he is~~ for glory, the more, like the ripe corn, they hang ~~he hangs~~ down their ~~his~~ head. The brighter and clearer is their ~~his~~ light, the more they see ~~he sees~~ of the shortcomings and infirmities of their ~~his~~ own heart. When first converted, they ~~he~~ would tell you they ~~he~~ saw but little of them compared to what they see ~~he sees~~ now. Would anyone know whether they are ~~he is~~ growing in grace? **Be sure that you look within for increased humility.**

Another mark of "growth in grace" is increased faith and love towards our Lord Jesus Christ.

The person ~~man~~ whose soul is "growing," finds more in Christ to rest upon every year, and rejoices more that they have ~~he has~~ such a Saviour. No doubt they ~~he~~ saw much in Him when first they ~~he~~ believed. Their ~~His~~ faith laid hold on the atonement of Christ and gave them ~~him~~ hope.

- But as they grow ~~he grows~~ in grace they see ~~he sees~~ a thousand things in Christ of which at first they ~~he~~ never dreamed. Their ~~His~~ love and power
- Their ~~His~~ heart and ~~His~~ intentions
- Their ~~His~~ offices as Substitute, Intercessor, Priest, Advocate, Physician, Shepherd, and Friend, unfold themselves to a growing soul in an unspeakable manner.

In short, they ~~he~~ discovers a suitableness in Christ to the wants of their ~~his~~ soul, of which the half was once not known to them ~~him~~. Would anyone know if they ~~he~~ is growing in grace? Then let them ~~him~~ look within for increased knowledge of Christ.

Another mark of "growth in grace" is increased holiness of life and conversation. The person ~~man~~ whose soul is "growing" gets more dominion over sin, the world, and the devil every year.

- They become ~~He becomes~~ more careful about their ~~his~~ temper, ~~his~~ words, and ~~his~~ actions.
- They are ~~He is~~ more watchful over their ~~his~~ conduct in every relation of life.
- They strive ~~He strives~~ more to be conformed to the image of Christ in all things, and to follow Him as their ~~his~~ example, as well as to trust in Him as his Savior ~~Saviour~~.
- They are ~~He is~~ not content with old attainments and former grace.

- They forget ~~He forgets~~ the things that are behind and reaches forth unto those things which are before, making "Higher!" "Upward!" "Forward!" "Onward!" his continual motto. "Brothers, I don't regard myself as yet having taken hold, but one thing I do: forgetting the things which are behind and stretching forward to the things which are before" (Philippians 3:13) ~~(Phil. iii. 13.)~~

- On earth they thirst and long ~~he thirsts and longs~~ to have a will more entirely in unison with God's will. In heaven the chief thing that they look ~~he looks~~ for, next to the presence of Christ, is complete separation from all sin. Would anyone know if they are ~~he is~~ growing in grace? Then let them ~~him~~ look within for increased holiness.

Another mark of "growth in grace" is increased spirituality of taste and mind.

The person ~~man~~ whose soul is "growing" takes more interest in spiritual things every year. They do ~~He does~~ not neglect their ~~his~~ duty in the world. They discharge ~~He discharges~~ faithfully, diligently, and conscientiously every relation of life, whether at home or abroad. But the things they love ~~he loves~~ best are spiritual things.

The ways, and fashions, and amusements, and recreations of the world have a continually decreasing place in their ~~his~~ heart. They do ~~He does~~ not condemn them as down right sinful, nor say that those who have anything to do with them are going to hell. They ~~He~~ only feel ~~feels~~ that they have a constantly diminishing hold on their ~~his~~ own affections, and gradually seem smaller and more trifling in their ~~his~~ eyes.

Spiritual companions, spiritual occupations, spiritual conversation, appear of ever-increasing value to them ~~him~~. Would anyone know if they are ~~he is~~ growing in grace? Then let them ~~him~~ look within for increasing spirituality of taste.

Another mark of "growth in grace" is increase of charity.

The person ~~man~~ whose soul is "growing" is more full of love every year - of love to all people ~~men~~, but especially of love towards the brethren. Their His love will show itself actively in a growing disposition to do kindnesses, to take trouble for others, to be good-natured to everybody, to be generous, sympathizing, thoughtful, tender-hearted, and considerate. It will show itself passively in a growing disposition to be meek and patient toward all people men, to put up with provocation and not stand upon rights, to bear and forbear much rather than quarrel.

A growing soul will try to put the best construction on other people's conduct, and to believe all things and hope all things, even to the end. There is no surer mark of backsliding and falling off in grace than an increasing disposition to find fault, pick holes, and see weak points in others. Would any one know if they are he is growing in grace? Then let them him look within for increasing charity.

One more mark of "growth in grace" is increased zeal and diligence in trying to do good to souls.

The person man who is really "growing" will take greater interest in the salvation of sinners every year. Missions at home and abroad, efforts to increase religious light and diminish religious darkness - all these things will every year have a greater place in their his attention. They He will not become "weary in well-doing" because they do he does not see every effort succeed.

They He will not care less for the progress of Christ's cause on earth as they he grows older, though they he will learn to expect less. They He will just work on, whatever the result may be - giving, praying, preaching, speaking, visiting, according to their his position - and count their his work its own reward.

One of the surest marks of spiritual decline is a decreased interest about the souls of others and the growth of Christ's kingdom. Would any one know whether they are he is growing in grace? Then let them him look within for increased concern about the salvation of souls.

Such are the most trustworthy marks of growth in grace. Let us examine them carefully, and consider what we know about them. I can well believe that they will not please some professing Christians in the present day. Those high -flying religionists, whose only notion of Christianity is that of a state of perpetual joy and ecstasy - who tell you that they have got far beyond the region of conflict and soul-humiliation - such persons no doubt will regard the marks I have laid down as "legal," "carnal," and "gendering to bondage." I cannot help that.

I call no person ~~man~~ master in these things. I only wish my statements to be tried in the balance of Scripture. And I firmly believe that what I have said is not only Scriptural, but agreeable to the experience of the most eminent saints in every age. Show me a person ~~man~~ in whom the six marks I have mentioned can be found. They are ~~He is~~ the person ~~man~~ who can give a satisfactory answer to the question, DO WE GROW?

MARKS OF Spiritual Growth

The third and last thing I propose to consider is this:

- The means that must be used by those who desire to grow in grace. The words of St. James must never be forgotten: "Every good gift and every perfect gift is from above, coming down from the Father of lights, with whom can be no variation nor turning shadow." (James 1:17) ~~(James i. 17.)~~

- This is no doubt as true of growth in grace as it is of everything else. It is the "gift of God." But still it must always be kept in mind that God is pleased to work by means. God has ordained means as well as ends. They ~~He~~ that would grow in grace must use the means of growth.

This is a point, I fear, which is too much overlooked by believers. Many admire growth in grace in others, and wish that they themselves were like them. But they seem to suppose that those who grow are what they are by some special gift or grant from God, and that as this gift is not bestowed on themselves they must be content to sit still. This is a grievous delusion, and one against which I desire to testify with all my might. I wish it to be distinctly understood that growth in grace is bound up with the use of means within the reach of all believers, and that, as a general rule, growing souls are what they are because they use these means.

Let me ask the special attention of my readers while I try to set forth in order the means of growth. Cast away forever the vain thought that if a believer does not grow in grace it is not their ~~his~~ fault. Settle it in your mind that a believer, a person ~~man~~ quickened by the Spirit, is not a mere dead creature, but a being or mighty capacities and responsibilities. Let the words of Solomon sink down into your heart: "The soul of the sluggard desires, and has nothing, but the desire of the diligent shall be fully satisfied." (Proverbs 13:4) ~~(Prov. xiii. 4.)~~

One thing essential to growth in grace is diligence in the use of private means of grace. By these I understand such means as a person ~~man~~ must use by themself ~~himself~~ alone, and no one can use for them ~~him~~.

I include under this head

- private prayer,

- private reading of the Scriptures,

- and private meditation

- and self-examination.

The person ~~man~~ who does not take pains about these three things must never expect to grow. Here are the roots of true Christianity. Wrong here, a person ~~man~~ is wrong all the way through! Here is the whole reason why many professing Christians never seem to get on. They are careless and messy ~~slovenly~~ about their private prayers. They read their Bibles but little, and with very little heartiness of spirit. They give themselves no time for self-inquiry and quiet thought about the state of their souls.

It is useless to conceal from ourselves that the age we live in is full of peculiar dangers. It is an age of great activity, and of much hurry, bustle, and excitement in religion. Many are "running to and fro," no doubt, and "knowledge is increased." "But you, Daniel, shut up the words and seal the book, even to the time of the end. Many will run back and forth, and knowledge will be increased." (Daniel 12:4) ~~(Dan. xii. 4.)~~

Thousands are ready enough for public meetings, sermon-hearing, or anything else in which there is "sensation." Few appear to remember the absolute necessity of making time to " Stand in awe, and don't sin. Search your own heart on your bed, and be still" (Psalm 4:4) (Psalm iv. 4.)

But without this there is seldom any deep spiritual prosperity. I suspect that English Christians two hundred years ago read their Bibles more, and were more frequently alone with God, than they are in the present day. Let us remember this point! Private religion must receive our first attention, if we wish our souls to grow.

Another thing which is essential to growth in grace is carefulness in the use of public means of grace.

By these I understand such means as a person man has within their his reach as a member of Christ's visible Church. Under this head I include

- the ordinances of regular Sunday worship,

- the uniting with God's people in common prayer and praise,

- the preaching of the Word,

- and the Sacrament of the Lord's Supper.

I firmly believe that the manner in which these public means of grace are used has much to say to the prosperity of a believer's soul. It is easy to use them in a cold and heartless way. The very familiarity of them is apt to make us careless. The regular return of the same voice, and the same kind of words, and the same ceremonies, is likely to make us sleepy, and callous, and unfeeling.

Here is a snare into which too many professing Christians fall. If we would grow we must be on our guard here. Here is a matter in which the Spirit is often grieved and saints take great damage. Let us strive to use the old prayers, and sing the old hymns, and kneel at the old communion-rail, and hear the old truths preached, with as much freshness and appetite as in the year we first believed.

It is a sign of bad health when a person loses relish for his food; and it is a sign of spiritual decline when we lose our appetite for means of grace. Whatever we do about public means, let us always do it "Whatever your hand finds to do, do it with your might; for there is no work, nor plan, nor knowledge, nor wisdom, in Sheol,† where you are going." (Ecclesiastes 9:10) (Eccles. ix. 10.) This is the way to grow!

Another thing essential to growth in grace is watchfulness over our conduct in the little matters of everyday life.

Our tempers, our tongues, the discharge of our several relations of life, our employment of time - each and all must be vigilantly attended to if we wish our souls to prosper.

Life is made up of days, and days of hours, and the little things of every hour are never so little as to be beneath the care of a Christian. When a tree begins to decay at root or heart, the mischief is first seen at the extreme end of the little branches. "He that despiseth little things," says an uninspired writer, "shall fall by little and little." That witness is true.

Let others despise us, if they like, and call us precise and over-careful. Let us patiently hold on our way, remembering that "we serve a precise God," that our Lord's example is to be copied in the least things as well as the greatest, and that we must "take up our cross daily" and hourly, rather than sin. We must aim to have a Christianity which, like the sap of a tree, runs through every twig and leaf of our character, and sanctifies all. This is one way to grow!

Another thing which is essential to growth in grace is caution about the company we keep and the friendships we form.

Nothing perhaps affects a persons man's character more than the company they keep he keeps. We catch the ways and tone of those we live and talk with, and unhappily get harm far more easily than good. Disease is infectious, but health is not.

Now if a professing Christian deliberately chooses to be intimate with those who are not friends of God and who cling to the world, their ~~his~~ soul is sure to take harm. <u>It is hard enough to serve Christ under any circumstances in such a world as this. But it is doubly hard to do it if we are friends of the thoughtless and ungodly.</u>

Mistakes in friendship or marriage-engagements are the whole reason why some have entirely ceased to grow.

"Don't be deceived! Evil companionships corrupt good morals." (1 Corinthians 15:33) ~~(1 Cor. xv. 33;)~~

"You adulterers and adulteresses, don't you know that friendship with the world is hostility toward God? Whoever therefore wants to be a friend of the world makes himself an enemy of God." (James 4:4) ~~(James iv. 4.)~~

Let us seek friends that will stir us up about

- our prayers,

- our Bible reading,

- and our employment of time

- about our souls,

- our salvation,

- and a world to come.

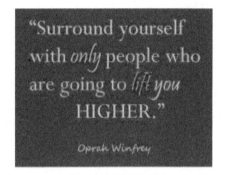

<u>Who can tell the good that a friend's word in season may do, or the harm that it may stop? This is one way to grow.</u>

There is one more thing which is absolutely essential to growth in grace - and that is regular and habitual communion with the Lord Jesus.

In saying this, let no one suppose for a minute that I am referring to the Lord's Supper. I mean nothing of the kind. I mean that daily habit of intercourse between the believer and their Savior ~~his Saviour~~, which can only be carried on by faith, prayer, and meditation. It is a habit, I fear, of which many believers know little.

A person ~~man~~ may be a believer and have their ~~his~~ feet on the rock, and yet live far below their ~~his~~ privileges. It is impossible to have "union" with Christ, and yet to have little if any "communion" with Him. But, for all that, there is such a thing.

The names and offices of Christ, as laid down in Scripture, appear to me to show unmistakably that this "communion" between the saint and their Savior his Saviour is not a mere fancy, but a real true thing.

- Between the "Bridegroom" and his bride
- between the "Head" and His members
- between the "Physician" and His patients
- between the "Advocate" and His clients
- between the "Shepherd" and His sheep
- between the "Master" and His scholars
- there is evidently implied a habit of familiar intercourse, of daily application for things needed, of daily pouring out and unburdening our hearts and minds.

Such a habit of dealing with Christ is clearly something more than a vague general trust in the work that Christ did for sinners. **It is getting close to Him, and laying hold on Him with confidence, as a loving, personal Friend. Tins is what I mean by communion.**

Now I believe that no person man will ever grow in grace who does not know something experimentally of the habit of "communion."

We must not be content with a general orthodox knowledge that justification is by faith and not by works, and that we put our trust in Christ.

We must go further than this. We must seek to have personal intimacy with the Lord Jesus, and to deal with Him as another man deals with a loving friend.

We must realize what it is to turn to Him first in

- every need,
- to talk to Him about every difficulty,
- to consult Him about every step,
- to spread before Him all our sorrows,
- to get Him to share in all our joys,
- to do all as in His sight,
- and to go through every day leaning on and looking to Him.

This is the way that St. Paul lived:

"I have been crucified with Christ, and it is no longer I who live, but Christ lives in me. That life which I now live in the flesh, I live by faith in the Son of God, who loved me and gave himself up for me." (Galatians 2:20) ~~(Gal. ii. 20)~~

"For to me to live is Christ, and to die is gain." (Philippians 1:21) ~~(Phil. i. 21.)~~

It is ignorance of this way of living that makes so many see no beauty in the book of hymn ~~Canticles~~. But it is the person ~~man~~ who lives in this way, who keeps up constant communion with Christ - this is the person ~~man~~, I say emphatically, whose soul will grow.

I leave the subject of growth in grace here. Far more might be said about it, if time permitted. But I have said enough, I hope, to convince my readers that the subject is one of vast importance. - Let me wind up all with some practical applications.

This book may fall into the hands of some who know nothing whatever about growth in grace. They have little or no concern about religion. A little proper Sunday church-going or chapel-going makes up the sum and substance of their Christianity. They are without spiritual life, and of course they cannot at present grow. <u>Are you one of these people?</u> **If you are, you are in a pitiable condition.**

Years are slipping away and time is flying.

Graveyards are filling up and families are thinning.

Death and judgment are getting nearer to us all.

And yet you live like one asleep about your soul! What madness! What folly! What suicide can be worse than this?

<u>Awake before it be too late</u>; awake, and arise from the dead, and live to God. Turn to Him who is sitting at the right hand of God, to be your Savior ~~Saviour~~ and Friend. Turn to Christ, and cry mightily to Him about your soul. There is yet hope!

He that called Lazarus from the grave is not changed.

He that commanded the widow's son at Nain to arise from his bier can do miracles yet for your soul.

<u>Seek Him at once: seek Christ, if you would not be lost for ever.</u>

Do not stand still talking, and meaning, and intending, and wishing, and hoping. Seek Christ that you may live, and that living you may grow.

This book may fall into the hands of some who ought to know something of growth in grace, but at present know nothing at all. They have made little or no progress since they were first converted. They seem to have "It will happen at that time, that I will search Jerusalem with lamps, and I will punish the men who are settled on their dregs, who say in their heart, "Yahweh will not do good, neither will he do evil."" (Zephaniah 1:12) ~~(Zep. i. 12.)~~

They go on from year to year content with

- old grace,
- old experience,
- old knowledge,
- old faith,
- old measure of attainment,
- old religious expressions,
- old set phrases.

Like the Gibeonites, their bread is always moldy ~~mouldy~~, and their shoes are patched and clouted. They never appear to get on. Are you one of these people? If you are, you are living far below your privileges and responsibilities. It is high time to examine yourself.

If you have reason to hope that you are a true believer and yet do not grow in grace, there must be a fault, and a serious fault somewhere. It cannot be the will of God that your soul should stand still.

- "But he gives more grace. Therefore it says, "God resists the proud, but gives grace to the humble."" (James 4:6) ~~(James iv. 6)~~

- He "Let those who favor my righteous cause shout for joy and be glad. Yes, let them say continually, "May Yahweh be magnified, who has pleasure in the prosperity of his servant!"" (Psalm 35:27) ~~(Ps. v. 27.)~~

It cannot be for your own happiness or usefulness that your soul should stand still. Without growth you will never rejoice in the Lord. "Rejoice in the Lord always! Again I will say, "Rejoice!"" (Philippians 4:4) (Phil. iv. 4.)

Without growth you will never do good to others. Surely this want of growth is a serious matter! It should raise in you great searchings of heart. There must be some "secret thing." "Are the consolations of God too small for you, even the word that is gentle toward you?" (Job 15:11) (Job xv. 11.) There must be some cause.

Take the advice I give you. Resolve this very day that you will find out the reason of your standstill condition. Probe with a faithful and firm hand every corner of your soul. Search from one end of the camp to the other, till you find out the Achan who is weakening your hands. Begin with an application to the Lord Jesus Christ, the great Physician of souls, and ask Him to heal the secret ailment within you, whatever it may be.

Begin as if you had never applied to Him before, and ask for grace to cut off the right hand and pluck out the right eye. But never, never be content, if your soul does not grow. For your peace sake, for your usefulness sake, for the honor honour of your Maker's cause, resolve to find out the reason why.

This book may fall into the hands of some who are really growing in grace, but are not aware of it, and will not allow it. Their very growth is the reason why they do not see their growth! Their continual increase in humility prevents them feeling that they get on.

Like Moses, when he came down from the mount from communing with God, their faces shine. And yet, like Moses, they are not aware of it.

Such Christians, I grant freely, are not common. But here and there such are to be found. Like angels' visits, they are few and far between. Happy is the neighborhood neighbourhood where such growing Christians live! To meet them and see them and be in their company, is like meeting and seeing a bit of "heaven upon earth."

Now what shall I say to such people?

What can I say?

What ought I to say?

Shall I bid them awake to a consciousness of their growth and be pleased with it?

I will do nothing of the kind. - Shall I tell them to plume themselves on their own attainments, and look at their own superiority to others? God forbid!

I will do nothing of the kind. - To tell them such things would do them no good. To tell them such things, above all, would be useless waste of time. If there is any one feature about a growing soul which specially marks them ~~him~~, it is his deep sense of their ~~his~~ own unworthiness.

They ~~He~~ never see ~~sees~~ anything to be praised in themself ~~himself~~. They ~~He~~ only feels that they are ~~he is~~ an unprofitable servant and the chief of sinners. It is the righteous, in the picture of the judgment -day, who say,

"Then the righteous will answer him, saying, 'Lord, when did we see you hungry and feed you, or thirsty and give you a drink?" (Matthew 25:37) ~~(Matt. xxv. 37.)~~

Extremes do indeed meet strangely sometimes. The conscience-hardened sinner and the eminent saint are in one respect singularly alike. Neither of them fully realizes his own condition. The one does not see their ~~his~~ own sin, nor the other their ~~his~~ own grace!

But shall I say nothing to growing Christians?

Is there no word of counsel I can address to them?

The sum and substance of all that I can say is to be found in two sentences: **"Go forward!" "Go on!"**

We can never have too much humility, too much faith in Christ, too much holiness, too much spirituality of mind, too much charity, too much zeal in doing good to others. Then let us be continually forgetting the things behind, and reaching forth unto the things before. "Brothers, I don't regard myself as yet having taken hold, but one thing I do: forgetting the things which are behind and stretching forward to the things which are before" (Philippians 3:13) ~~(Phil. iii. 13.)~~

The best of Christians in these matters is infinitely below the perfect pattern of their ~~his~~ Lord. Whatever the world may please to say, we may be sure there is no danger of any of us becoming "too good."

Let us cast to the winds as idle talk the common notion that it is possible to be "extreme" and go "too far" in religion. This is a favorite ~~favourite~~ He of the devil, and one which he circulates with vast industry. No doubt there are enthusiasts and fanatics to be found who bring evil report upon Christianity by their extravagances and follies. But if any one means to say that a mortal person ~~man~~ can be too humble, too charitable, too holy, or too diligent in doing good, they ~~he~~ must either be an infidel or a fool. In serving pleasure and money it is easy to go too far. But in following the things which make up true religion, and in serving Christ there can be no extreme.

Let us never measure our religion by that of others, and think we are doing enough if we have gone beyond our neighbors ~~neighbours~~. This is another snare of the devil. Let us mind our own business. "What is that to thee?" said our Master on a certain occasion:

"Jesus said to him, "If I desire that he stay until I come, what is that to you? You follow me." (John 21:22) ~~(John xxi. 22.)~~

Let us follow on, aiming at nothing short of perfection.

Let us follow on, making Christ's life and character our only pattern and example.

Let us follow on, remembering daily that at our best we are miserable sinners.

Let us follow on, and never forget that it signifies nothing whether we are better than others or not.

At our very best we are far worse than we ought to be. <u>There will always be room for improvement in us.</u> We shall be debtors to Christ's mercy and grace to the very last. Then let us leave off looking at others and comparing ourselves with others. We shall find enough to do if we look at our own hearts.

Last, but not least, if we know anything of growth in grace, and desire to know more, let us not be surprised if we have to go through much trial and affliction in this world.

I firmly believe it is the experience of nearly all the most eminent saints. Like their blessed Master they have been

"He was despised and rejected by men, a man of suffering and acquainted with disease. He was despised as one from whom men hide their face; and we didn't respect him." (Isaiah 53:3) (Isa. liii. 3)

and " For it became him, for whom are all things and through whom are all things, in bringing many children to glory, to make the author of their salvation perfect through sufferings." (Hebrews 2:10) (Heb. ii. 10.)

It is a striking saying of our Lord, "Every branch in me that doesn't bear fruit, he takes away. Every branch that bears fruit, he prunes, that it may bear more fruit." (John 15:2) (John xv. 2.)

It is a melancholy fact, that constant temporal prosperity, as a general rule, is injurious to a believer's soul. We cannot stand it.

Sickness, and losses, and crosses, and anxieties, and disappointments seem absolutely needful to keep us humble, watchful, and spiritual-minded.

They are as needful as the pruning knife to the vine, and the refiner's furnace to the gold.

They are not pleasant to flesh and blood. We do not like them, and often do not see their meaning. "All chastening seems for the present to be not joyous but grievous; yet afterward it yields the peaceful fruit of righteousness to those who have been trained by it." (Hebrews 12:11) (Heb. xii. 11.)

We shall find that all worked for our good when we reach heaven. Let these thoughts abide in our minds, if we love growth in grace.

When days of darkness come upon us, let us not count it a strange thing. Rather let us remember that lessons are learned on such days which would never have been learned in sunshine.

Let us say to ourselves, "**This also is for my profit, that I may be a partaker of God's holiness. It is sent in love. I am in**

God's best school. Correction is instruction. This is meant to make me grow."

I leave the subject of growth in grace here. I trust I have said enough to set some readers thinking about it. All things are growing older:

- the world is growing old;
- we ourselves are grow-older.
- A few more summers,
- a few more winters,
- a few more sicknesses,
- a few more sorrows,
- a few more weddings,
- a few more funerals,
- a few more meetings,
- and a few more partings, and then - what?

Why the grass will be growing over our graves!

Now would it not be well to look within, and put to our souls a simple question? In religion, in the things that concern our peace, in the great matter of personal holiness, are we getting on? **DO WE GROW?**

True grace is progressive, of a spreading, growing nature. It is with grace as it is with light: first, there is the day-break; then it shines brighter to the full noon -day. <u>The saints are not only compared to stars for their light, but to trees for their growth.</u>

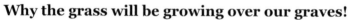

"to provide for those who mourn in Zion, to give to them a garland for ashes, the oil of joy for mourning, the garment of praise for the spirit of heaviness, that they may be called trees of righteousness, the planting of Yahweh, that he may be glorified." (Isaiah 61:3) (Isa. lxi. 3;

" I will be like the dew to Israel. He will blossom like the lily, and send down his roots like Lebanon." (Hosea 14:5) (Hos. xiv. 5.)

A good Christian is not like Hezekiah's sun that went backwards, nor Joshua's sun that stood still, but is always advancing in holiness, and increasing with the increase of God." - Thomas Watson, Minister of St. Stephen's Walbrook, 1660. (Body of Divinity.)

"The growth of grace is the best evidence of the truth of grace. Things that have not life will not grow. A picture will not grow. A stake in a hedge will not grow. But a plant that hath vegetative life will grow. The growing of grace shows it to be alive in the soul." - T. Watson, 1660.

"Christian, as ever you would stir up others to exalt the God of grace, look to the exercise and improvement of your own graces. When poor servants live in a family, and see the faith, and love, and wisdom, and patience, and humility of a master, shining like the stars in heaven, it draws forth their hearts to bless the Lord that ever they came into such a family. When men's graces shine as Moses' face did, when their life, as one speaketh of Joseph's life, is a very heaven, sparkling with virtues as so many bright stars, how much others are stirred up to glorify God, and cry, 'These are Christians indeed! these are an honour to their God, a crown to their Christ, and a credit to their Gospel! Oh, if they were all such, we would be Christians too!" - T. Brooks, 1661. (Unsearchable Riches.)

"The right manner of growth is to grow less in one's own eyes. 'I am a worm and no man.' (Psa. xxii. 6.) The sight of corruption and ignorance makes a Christian grow into a dislike of himself. He doth vanish in his own eyes. Job abhorred himself in the dust. (Job xlii. 6.) This is good, to grow out of conceit with oneself." - T. Watson. 1660.

"It is a sign of not growing in grace, when we are less troubled about sin. Time was when the least sin did grieve us (as the least hair makes the eye weep), but now we can digest sin without remorse. Time was when a Christian was troubled if he neglected closet prayer; now he can omit family prayer. Time was when vain thoughts did not trouble him; now he is not troubled for loose practices. There is a sad declension in religion; and grace is so far from growing that we can hardly perceive its puke to beat." - T. Watson. 1660.

"If now you would be rich in graces, look to your walking. It is not the knowing soul, nor the talking soul, but the close -walking soul, the obedient soul, that is rich. Others may be rich in notions, but none so rich in spiritual experience, and in all holy and heavenly graces, as close -walking Christians." - T. Brooks. 1661.

"It is a sign of not growing in grace, when we grow more worldly. Perhaps once we were mounted into higher orbits, we did set our hearts on things above, and speak the language of Canaan. But now our minds are taken off heaven, we dig our comforts out of these lower mines, and with Satan compass the earth. It is a sign we are going down hill apace, and our grace is in a consumption. It is observable when nature decays, and people are near dying, they grow more stooping. And truly when men's hearts grow more stooping to the earth, and they can hardly lift up themselves to an heavenly t hought, if grace be not dead, yet it is ready to die." - T. Watson. 1660.

"Experience will tell every Christian that the more strictly, and closely, and constantly he walketh with God, the stronger he groweth in duty. Infused habits are advantaged by exercise. As the fire that kindled the wood for sacrifices upon the altar first came down from heaven, but then was to be kept alive by the care and labour of the priests, so the habits of spiritual grace are indeed in-fused from God, and must be maintained by daily influences from God, yet with a concurrence also of our own labours, in waiting upon God, and exercising ourselves with godliness; and the more a Christian doth so exercise himself, the more strong he shall grow." - Collinges on Providence. 1678.

"Let them be thy choicest companions, that have made Christ their chiefest companion. Do not so much eye the outsides of men as their inside: look most to their internal worth. Many persons have their eyes upon the external garb of a professor. But give me a Christian that minds the internal worth of persons, that makes such as are most filled with the fulness of God his choicest and chiefest companions." - T. Brooks. 1661.

"Christians may be growing when they think they do not grow."
'There is that maketh himself poor, yet he is rich.' (Prov. xiii. 7.)
The sight that Christians have of their defects in grace, and their
thirst after greater measures of grace, makes them think they do
not grow. He who covets a great estate, because he hath not so
much as he desires thinks himself poor." - T. Watson. 1660.

"Souls may be rich in grace, and yet not know it, not perceive it.
The child is heir to a crown or a great estate, but knows it not.
Moses' face did shine, and others saw it, but he perceived it not. So
many a precious soul is rich in grace, and others see it, and know
it, and bless God for it, and yet the poor soul perceives it not. -
Sometimes this arises from the soul's strong desires of spiritual
riches. The strength of the soul's desires after spiritual riches doth
often take away the very sense of growing spiritually rich. Many
covetous men's desires are so strongly carried forth after earthly
riches, that though they do grow rich, yet they cannot perceive it,
they cannot believe it. It is just so with many a precious Christian:
his desires after spiritual riches are so strong, that they take away
the very sense of his growing rich in spirituals. Many Christians
have much worth within them, but they see it not. It was a good
man that said, 'The Lord was in this place and I knew it not.' -
Again, this ariseth sometimes from men neglecting to cast up their
accounts. Many men thrive and grow rich, and yet, by neglecting
to cast up their accounts, they cannot tell whether they go forward
or backward. It is so with many precious souls. Again, this ariseth
sometimes from the soul's too frequent casting up of its accounts.
If a man should cast up his accounts once a week, or once a month,
he may not be able to discern that he doth grow rich, and yet he
may grow rich. But let him compare one year with another, and he
shall clearly see that he doth grow rich. - Again, this sometimes
ariseth from the soul's mistakes in casting up its accounts. The
soul many times mistakes: it is in a hurry, and then it puts down
ten for a hundred, and a hundred for a thousand. Look, as hyp-
ocrites put down their counters for gold, their pence for pounds,
and always prize themselves above the market, so sincere souls do
often put down their pounds for pence, their thousands for hundreds, and still prize themselves below the market." - Thomas
Brooks. 1661. (Unsearchable Riches)

Printed in Great Britain
by Amazon

39851698R00050